APR 1 0 2015

P9-CCZ-971

AMERICAN

MADE

AMERICAN MADE

WHY MAKING THINGS WILL
RETURN US TO GREATNESS

DAN DIMICCO

palgrave
macmillan

AMERICAN MADE
Copyright © Dan DiMicco, 2015.
All rights reserved.

First published in 2015 by PALGRAVE MACMILLAN® TRADE in the United
States—a division of St. Martin's Press LLC, 175 Fifth Avenue, New York, NY
10010.

Palgrave® and Macmillan® are registered trademarks in the United States,
the United Kingdom, Europe and other countries.

ISBN 978-1-137-27979-8

Library of Congress Cataloging-in-Publication Data

DiMicco, Dan.
    American made : why making things will return us to greatness / Dan
DiMicco ; introduction by David Rothkopf.
  pages   cm
    ISBN 978-1-137-27979-8 (hardback)
    1. Manufacturing industries—United States. 2. Industrial policy—United
States. 3. Job creation—United States. 4. United States—Economic policy.
I. Title.
HD9725.D56   2015
338.4'7670973—dc23

                                                                2014030410

Design by Letra Libre, Inc.

First edition: March 2015

10 9 8 7 6 5 4 3 2

Printed in the United States of America.

CONTENTS

INTRODUCTION

"NEVER SAY NEVER"

David Rothkopf

THE UNITED STATES FINDS ITSELF AT A CRITICAL juncture. Six years after the Great Recession began, millions of Americans still struggle with one of the weakest economic recoveries in a century. Job growth remains anemic, and wage growth for American workers remains low; in fact, wages are only up about 2 percent compared to a year ago, down from their 20-year prerecession average growth rate of 3.2 percent. Yet, at the same time, Wall Street—which helped precipitate the downturn—is doing quite well. Both the Dow Jones Industrial Average and the S&P 500 shattered prerecession record highs in early 2013 and have continued to rise. And the banks that were "too big to fail" just a few years ago are going strong once again.

Something is broken in the economy.

The United States lost 8.2 million jobs in the last recession. Since January 2010, when the economy gradually began to show renewed signs of life, we have only succeeded in gaining those initial lost jobs back. During Barack Obama's first term in office, which includes 2009 when job losses were at their absolute worst, just 1.2 million nonfarm payroll jobs were recovered.

Although the official unemployment rate has fallen from its recession high of 10.2 percent to 5.9 percent, the "real" rate—the unemployed plus those involuntarily working part-time or who are marginally attached to the labor force—remains near 12 percent. Almost the entire decline in unemployment can be explained by millions of people who have dropped out of the workforce entirely. The labor participation rate in September 2014 was 63 percent, lower than at any time since the terrible double-dip recession of 1980–81. These are people who aren't working or even looking for work. Some of them are retirees. Many more are able-bodied Americans in the prime of their working lives who have simply given up.

But the ills afflicting the U.S. economy cannot be blamed solely on the ravages of the Great Recession. Beyond the millions of jobs the recession swept away, the United States has lost 5.2 million manufacturing jobs since 2000. Only about one-third of those jobs were lost since 2008. During the height of the recession, more than 2 million construction workers were idle. Five years later, unemployment in the construction sector remained high at over 12 percent.

In the midst of this crisis, many Americans looked to the government for answers. What they found was dysfunction, bickering, and a seemingly unending series of distractions.

Clearly, something is broken in government too.

Under these circumstances, where can Americans look for insight and vision? The solution has to be in the private sector. But it won't be in the financial services industry, the big banks and the Wall Street brokerages that did so much harm to the economy. And it won't be in the large multinational corporations that have sought record profits by shipping jobs overseas. It is in a surprising place: U.S. manufacturing, which by all accounts is an endangered species.

Enter Dan DiMicco. From 2000 until December 2012, DiMicco was chief executive officer of Nucor, the largest U.S. steel producer by volume and the largest recycler in North America. He remains chairman emeritus of the company. I knew DiMicco as an outspoken executive who not only revived a major U.S. manufacturing firm during extremely challenging economic times, but who also helped galvanize the flagging steel industry when many companies were in bankruptcy or headed overseas. With some 22,000 employees at plants across the United States, Nucor has the distinction of being one of the few large American manufacturers that emerged from the recession stronger than when the crisis began—and without a single layoff. In a nation where many economists and experts have written off American manufacturing as a thing of the past, DiMicco and Nucor have shown that a forward-looking company can not only survive but flourish, even in dismal times.

How did DiMicco pull it off? What does he know that so many other executives and experts apparently do not? What lessons could he impart to a country that seems resigned to high unemployment and tepid economic growth as "the new normal"?

I wanted to know. So I sat down with DiMicco at Nucor's head-quarters in Charlotte, North Carolina, to ask a few questions—most importantly, how he thought the United States found itself in its present predicament, and what he believes the country should do to get out of it. Those initial questions soon evolved into a series of deep conversations about the U.S. economy, American competitiveness, and the heart of the problem: our current jobs crisis. Those conversations, which stretched out over nearly two years, became the backbone of the book you're reading now.

I began thinking of our talks as "conversations with an American industrialist." That word, *industrialist,* may sound like a throwback to a bygone era, but not so. Not quite. American industrialists are fewer in number than they were 50 or 100 years ago, but they are no less important. When we think of industrialists, we often think of pioneers, innovators—people of vision like Henry Ford, Charles Dana, and Henry Kaiser. I think DiMicco fits that bill. He is, in fact, the quintessential twenty-first-century American industrialist.

Given Nucor's success in the face of a highly competitive global marketplace and nearly unprecedented economic circumstances, DiMicco lends a unique and optimistic voice to the current conversation. When DiMicco speaks—and he is a frequent guest on cable business news channels—one immediately gets the impression of a working-class man who isn't at all afraid to get his hands dirty. He *looks* and *sounds* like a steelworker: stocky, no-nonsense, perfectly blunt. But it also quickly becomes clear, as he discusses the economic crisis or the postwar history of American manufacturing, that this is a man of keen intellect and insight. It probably doesn't hurt that he has engineering degrees from Brown and the University of Pennsylvania. This is a man who is as comfortable conversing with U.S. presidents as he is chatting with welders.

DiMicco is worth paying attention to precisely *because* he rejects the current conventional wisdom about the economy, jobs, and the future of American manufacturing, much as Nucor bucked the conventional wisdom when it entered the steel business in the 1960s. "If I've learned anything over the past 30 years, it's that you should never say never," DiMicco says. "What may look impossible or simply not viable today could be the next big thing tomorrow. You just don't know what changes are coming, and if you want to compete and survive and grow, you can't rule out any possibilities."

It's a view informed by his upbringing and education. Growing up in Mount Kisco, New York, DiMicco says he never imagined he would become a steel man. He certainly never imagined he would be CEO of one of the nation's most innovative manufacturers. Instead, he wanted to build rockets for NASA. "When I was studying metallurgy at Brown in the early 1970s, all of my engineering buddies and I sat around laughing that steel was a dinosaur industry headed for extinction," he says. "Boy, were we ever wrong!"

After DiMicco graduated from Brown and earned his master's degree in engineering from UPenn, he discovered NASA wasn't hiring. With a wife to care for and their first child on the way, he went to work instead at the research and development department at Republic Steel in Ohio. DiMicco recalls Republic as a fine company to embark on a career, but "not really a place you wanted to finish it." After a few years on the job, it became clear the company was too bureaucratic and stifling for DiMicco, who was looking for more interesting challenges. "I worked with a lot of really smart, capable people," he says, "but they just seemed stuck in a rut."

"At the time, I remember how Nucor, this upstart company, kept appearing in all the trade journals," DiMicco continues. This was in the late 1970s, when the U.S. steel industry was struggling to compete with Japan, and the larger, integrated companies were shutting down mills and laying off workers by the thousands. The outlook was bleak. "Here was this company that started out with two mills churning out joists, and they're building new plants, expanding into new markets, and had never laid off a single worker in its history," he recalls. One magazine featured Nucor on its cover with the headline, "The Little Steel Mill That Could."[1] "I would read stories like that, then I would listen to these guys I worked with say Nucor would never last; they're just in the rebar business; they'll never be able to catch up with the bigs. And hearing all of that negativity made me think, *You know, maybe Nucor is more my kind of place.*"

In 1982, when the chief metallurgist's position opened up at a new Nucor mill in Plymouth, Utah, DiMicco applied for the job and got it. That same year, this company that was never supposed to succeed broke into the top ten largest steel producers in the United States. DiMicco spent nearly a decade in Plymouth, where he worked his way up to manager of the plant's melt shop, a post he held for four years. "I loved every minute of it. I worked a lot of hard hours and had to make my way because everybody was skeptical that I could be a leader and help them to improve," he says.

But his efforts soon caught the eye of Nucor's executive team in North Carolina. DiMicco was promoted again in 1990, this time to general manager of the plant Nucor jointly owned and operated with Japan's Yamato Kogyo Company in Blytheville, Arkansas. "I never focused on becoming a general manager," DiMicco says. "I was focused on being the best melt shop manager that I could be, the best in the company. I always had been taught whatever opportunity you're given, just give it everything you have, and people will know. If you're in a good company, people will notice. And when they're looking for somebody to take on new responsibilities, they'll knock on your door, and you'll get the opportunity. And Nucor was that kind of company."

DiMicco spent nine record-setting years in Arkansas, during which time he nearly tripled the size of the Nucor-Yamato plant and solidified his leadership style. When his next promotion came in 1999, it was to executive vice president, a position he held for a year before Nucor's board of directors named him CEO in 2000.

As a young manager in Utah, and later as a general manager in Arkansas, DiMicco quickly came to know Nucor's legendary CEO, Ken Iverson, who is rightly held up alongside Andrew Carnegie as a titan among American industrialists and one of the steel industry's greatest innovators. Iverson, who retired in 1996 and died in 2002, took a failing nuclear technology company and transformed it into a steelmaking powerhouse. When Iverson took over as company president in 1965, Nucor was still called the Nuclear Corporation of America. (The name didn't officially change until 1971.) At the time, its core businesses included making radiation-detection instruments and developing exotic minerals for industrial use. But the company was losing money in every division except one: Vulcraft, which made steel joists used in buildings. Iverson's mandate from Nuclear's board of directors was to get the company out of the red. He assembled a top-notch team, shed the unprofitable parts of the business, and built a culture that rewarded autonomy, creativity, clear communication, and productivity.

"Ken's whole business philosophy boiled down to having a long-term approach," DiMicco says. "He knew a lot of the large manufacturers were unionized and heavily bureaucratic. They had terrible communication and people who were rewarded for how long they'd been with the company rather than their ability to get a job done. Ken's idea was to put together a nimble organization that could do with less than everybody else, yet still be successful."

And so the concept of pay for performance came into play. Nucor has never offered lavish salaries, and the company is studiously non-union. Yet Nucor's compensation is well above the industry average. Everyone at the company—from entry level to executive—has a chance to earn regular bonuses based on performance. The more productive a crew is at rolling out steel during its shift, the more people take home in their next paycheck. DiMicco's own compensation as CEO and board chairman depended in large part on earnings and how well Nucor's stock performed. When the Great Recession struck in 2008 and Nucor's revenues fell, everyone felt the pain—including DiMicco. But pay for performance remained critical to the company's culture, because it creates an environment where teamwork becomes paramount. As DiMicco tells it, "Ken wanted a company where an individual would be rewarded over time for his team's accomplishments, not by how well a guy played golf with the boss or how many years he clocked in on time."

Also critical to Nucor's long-term success, DiMicco explains, was the company's practice of no layoffs. Nucor hasn't laid off a single employee in more than 40 years, not even during the last recession, when the pressure was overwhelming. DiMicco explains: "The reason for that is pretty simple. Keeping your people employed builds trust. It builds long-term loyalty and a genuine sense of ownership in the company. And the payback on that is far better than if you say, 'Times are tough, we don't need you anymore, but thanks for all the good work you did for us. We will call you when things get better . . . maybe.'"

DiMicco says perhaps the most important lesson Iverson conveyed during his three-decade tenure as CEO was that no problem is unsolvable. "Every time some industry critic said we'd fail, or we couldn't make a new process work, or that we would never be able to compete in some new market, Ken and the rest of us took that as a challenge and an opportunity," he says.

In the 1980s, for example, Nucor was looking for a cost-effective way of entering the flat-rolled steel market. Flat-rolled steel is used in everything from small household appliances to automobiles, and it was very costly and labor-intensive to produce. Nucor's engineers spent several years studying how it could be done. By 1989, Nucor took a risk on thin-slab casting, which was a new process that hadn't been commercially viable before then. Nucor spent $270 million building a state-of-the-art mill in Crawfordsville, Indiana. *Forbes* called the move "Nucor's boldest gamble."[2] DiMicco remembers it well. "The big steel companies said we'd never pull it off. Bethlehem Steel in particular sent around memos explaining to its customers why our new process could never succeed," he recalls. "Today, of course, we're one of the top producers of flat-rolled steel in America, and Bethlehem is out of business."

In Nucor's corporate culture, "never say never" is a kind of mantra. "It suits our approach to innovation and risk-taking very well," DiMicco says. "If somebody says something can't be done, our response has always been, 'Get out of the way so we can do it.' Because if we can do it, that creates a huge competitive advantage for us. Nucor succeeded by doing the sort of stuff so-called experts said we could never do." DiMicco applies that same "never say never" ethos to the broader American economy. "When people say, 'Well, manufacturing is dead in this country and it's never coming back,' or 'We can do just fine as a service-oriented economy,' statements like that are completely foreign to my way of thinking. They bear absolutely no relation to the way America has traditionally done business."

Although DiMicco doesn't think the government alone has all of the solutions for the nation's economic woes, he believes elected officials' tendency to engage in petty partisan squabbles has led not only to needless pain and suffering—especially among the middle class—but also drags down recovery and growth. This is nothing less than a failure of leadership. "I understand the politician's instinct to get by until the next election, but I don't accept it," he told me during one of our first meetings. "We solved an infinite number of problems as Nucor was growing. We solve countless problems every day. The problem America faces now is really no different, if you think about it clearly and logically. We can fix it—but only if we confront the problem for what it is, not for what we want it to be."

DiMicco paused, then added, "That's what good leaders do."

THE NATURE OF THE PROBLEM:
BEYOND THE GREAT RECESSION

This book is a distillation of several conversations about good leadership, about solving an existential crisis, and about mapping the road back to robust economic growth and middle-class prosperity.

First, the diagnosis. DiMicco says the problem America has today is straightforward: the economy's job-creation engine is broken, and the country is not creating the sorts of jobs that generate real, tangible wealth. In chapter 1, DiMicco explains the historic scale of the economic crisis, in particular how America's current leadership has failed to define the crisis correctly. He parts ways with the Republican leaders in Congress who say the greatest threat to American prosperity is excessive spending and the national debt, arguing that the best way to overcome the federal budget deficit and pay down the debt is to first put the country back on track toward being a global leader in manufacturing.

"Manufacturing should not be minimized," he says. "It should be *maximized*."

If America is going to overcome the current economic crisis, we need a much better understanding of how the nation got into the crisis in the first place. The problem goes well beyond a few election cycles. In chapter 2, DiMicco offers his view of history, explaining how far the United States moved from being the nation that rebuilt Europe and Japan after World War II, put a man on the moon, and kept the threat of Soviet communism at bay. It wasn't just a response to a threat from an unfriendly adversary. "We had leaders who offered a superior vision for the future," he says. "We're missing those leaders today."

Another reason the United States is struggling to put people back to work is that our current political leadership continues to ignore a fundamental issue: trade-distorting policies and practices. As DiMicco explains in chapter 3, America's trade problem started with some short-sighted decisions after World War II, when the United States was riding high. Some of those decisions might have made sense in the short term, but made less sense as time wore on. Mistaking short-term remedies for long-term policy proved a recipe for disaster. DiMicco argues that we've been dealing—or, rather, *not* dealing—with those mistakes ever since.

"For 30 years," he says, "we've supported an economic model and trade policies that say we could cease being a nation that creates, makes, and builds things, and become instead a nation that just services things—and not only could we remain prosperous, we could grow richer. Sorry, that isn't the way the world works." All of the staggering wealth that was supposedly created in the 1990s and 2000s—think of the $7.3 trillion in home equity that evaporated when the housing bubble burst—wasn't really created at all. In DiMicco's words, "it was a shell game."

"What did we get by playing that game? We got bubbles. The savings-and-loan bubble, the dot-com bubble, the Enron bubble, the housing bubble, all of the Ponzi schemes originating on Wall Street, one after another, all trying to create wealth from nothing, all driven by major debt and smoke and mirrors."

Instead of allowing ourselves to wander further down the path of exploding bubbles and phantom prosperity, DiMicco argues that the nation's political and economic leaders should have focused on *innovating, building, and making things.* "We're kidding ourselves if we think the U.S. economy will come back using an obviously discredited model," he says. "We won't recover with a more-of-the-same approach. The politicians and economists who bought into that other model were wrong. People today who say we don't need to be manufacturers or makers and builders of things are still wrong. They haven't learned." By shifting from policies that create real wealth to policies that glorify false wealth, the distortions in the economy that followed caused American manufacturing to decline from 20 percent of U.S. gross domestic product in the 1980s to just 12.5 percent today.

In chapter 4, DiMicco delves deeper into why the talk in the media and in Congress isn't really serious about creating jobs. Political leaders continue to define the problem as something smaller than it really is, and most of the talk we've heard about jobs in the past six years is lip service from people interested only in winning elections.

Unlike many CEOs of Fortune 500 companies, DiMicco takes issue with aspects of globalization and free trade, two trends that have dominated the political and economic landscape for a generation. His assessment of free trade, which he spells out in chapter 5, is characteristically blunt: "Free trade is wonderful in theory, but it doesn't work. It is an academic luxury that the real world doesn't enjoy. If you want to study it at Harvard or Chicago, be my guest. But understand that global trade today is anything but free."

For those of us who've made the case for the advantages of free trade over the past 20 years or so, DiMicco's argument, at first blush, may smack of old-fashioned protectionism. But he convincingly denies the charge. "I'm not a protectionist," he says. "I maintain that free trade has no application when other countries—and not just China, by the way—refuse to play by the rules, subsidize their export industries, and manipulate their currencies to get an unfair competitive advantage."

Instead, DiMicco argues that for free trade to work, it must be rules-based. And for the United States to be a major exporter in the world, it requires a trading system that can effectively police what he calls "predatory, mercantilistic trading practices," such as the illegal dumping[3] of steel and other commodities coming into the country.

DiMicco's refreshing heterodoxy isn't limited only to trade. In chapter 6, he takes aim at the prevailing conventional wisdom surrounding the so-called knowledge economy and the skills gap, which was a prominent issue in the 2012 presidential debates. While innovation is important—crucial, in fact—DiMicco posits that it is not enough to generate real economic growth. And the fact is, more often than not, the supposed value created in the knowledge economy doesn't stay in the United States. "It's no accident that just as manufacturing has moved offshore, our research and development is now following," he says. "If we use a little common sense, we'll quickly realize that if the United States doesn't make what it innovates, soon enough we'll lose our ability to innovate, too."

As for the skills gap, while America's public education system may require fundamental reforms, businesses have always had a skills gap that they adjust to. "Technology changes, processes change," DiMicco says. "That happens every decade. This time is no different."

What *is* different, he contends, is an ill-founded belief that training can bridge gaps that are much wider than before and are growing at faster rates. DiMicco believes the answer isn't to create additional government training programs—those are almost always a waste of money and fail to meet their goals. Most skills in manufacturing and construction can be taught on the job. That's how businesses have done it for decades, and how many businesses—including Nucor—do it today. But part of the problem now, DiMicco says, is that while business has always found ways to address skills gaps created by changing technology, manufacturing has also been hurt by a changing culture.

"It isn't just engineers we are having trouble finding, it's electricians and welders, too," he explains. "People have been saying for years that the manufacturing sector is dead and the future lies in the service economy. What parent would want their child to be a welder or electrician when they are repeatedly told manufacturing is dead? Well, it is not dead and we need these skills." The need to fill those jobs in the manufacturing sector will spur people to acquire the right skills, but changing the culture will take time. "This is a problem 30 years in the making," DiMicco says.

But private enterprise can only do so much before it runs into state-imposed barriers. Government really is making the jobs crisis worse and hurting economic growth, as DiMicco articulates in chapter 7. Remember the $787 billion stimulus President Obama passed in his first weeks in office? It failed, DiMicco contends, not because the government spent too little, but because the money was *spent badly*. Only $60 billion—less than 8 percent—of the stimulus was allocated to infrastructure work, where it would have had the greatest possible multiplying effect. In fact, only half of the stimulus money Congress earmarked for roads, bridges, and other improvements was actually spent because states either wouldn't or couldn't come up with federally mandated matching funds. What's more, 80 percent of the stimulus was spent on goods and services outside of the United States, making a minimal impact on our economy. At the same time, federal and state regulators have been working overtime to devise new regulations that DiMicco says is undermining the ability of manufacturers to create new jobs.

THE WAY BACK

So how should the United States go about creating jobs—as many as 30 million new jobs by 2025? It requires a national policy that invests in the future, with sensible regulations that promote growth and rules-based, enforced free trade, all while generating new revenue for the government. In the concluding chapters of the book, DiMicco articulates an expansive vision of how that would work in practice.

To begin, DiMicco says we need to rebuild the backbone of the U.S. economy. That means investing heavily in America's infrastructure, as he lays out in chapter 8. These are not make-work jobs or "bridges to nowhere." The United States has a bona fide need for at least $3.6 trillion in infrastructure improvements and expansion by 2020. This includes everything from repaving the half-century-old interstate highway system and buttressing an overtaxed power grid to updating an antiquated air-traffic control system, repairing aging dams, and plugging leaky waterways. "It's going to be expensive," he says, "and we'll need to take on some debt to fix everything that needs fixing." But DiMicco argues the work is essential and the improvements will pay dividends in the long run. It can be done, he says, through the kind of public-private partnerships that helped America win World War II and put Neil Armstrong on the moon.

Then in chapter 9, DiMicco makes the case for expanding U.S. domestic energy resources. Natural gas can be a real game changer for American manufacturing. It isn't just about weaning the United States from foreign oil pumped out of the desert in increasingly hostile countries. We import plenty of oil from our friends and neighbors, Canada and Mexico. In fact, as DiMicco points out, energy makes up about 50 percent of the $475 billion annual U.S. trade deficit. "Imagine what we could do by developing domestic sources of shale and natural gas," he says. "We could cut energy costs for manufacturers. That would lower the price of goods Americans buy, boost our competitive advantage with other countries, and create millions of jobs in the process. What's not to like?"

But in order for that to happen, the United States needs a new energy policy. DiMicco favors an "all of the above approach" that includes other energy resources, including wind and solar, but also nuclear power. But he doesn't believe it's feasible to "decarbonize" the U.S. economy anytime soon.

Government can encourage all of this without picking winners and losers or taxing less-favored sources of energy out of existence. Spurring energy development must go hand in hand with revitalizing American manufacturing. As DiMicco explains in chapter 10, creating real wealth is the only path back to full employment.

There are some signs of a manufacturing renaissance in the United States, owing to a growing disenchantment with China and the natural gas boom here at home. But it's early yet. In order for that nascent renaissance to reach full flower, DiMicco says state and federal governments must unburden business and manufacturing from the regulations and permitting hurdles that have been pouring down on them for years.

As much as anything else, perhaps what the United States needs today is an attitude adjustment—or at least a fresh perspective.

DiMicco is passionate when he talks about galvanizing the American job-creation engine. "We have to be an economy that makes things, builds things, innovates, and services those sectors," he says. "We can't just be a service-oriented economy. We can't just be consumers. We must *produce*."

If the problem stems from the failure of America's leadership to envision the kind of economy that we should have, then a large part of the solution requires new voices, and new leaders. The economy America needs is a create-and-build economy. We've had it before; we can regenerate it. With prudent investments in key areas—the trade deficit, energy, infrastructure—the jobs would follow. The system is equipped basically to generate those jobs in a matter of just a few years, if we're willing to undertake the effort.

DiMicco is not shy about saying that if America's leaders would adopt Nucor's philosophy and way of doing business, the country would be in considerably better shape. I ask whether he's confident such an effort would be successful, despite the challenges posed by the current political leadership and interests wed to the economic status quo.

"Absolutely," he replies. "You know why? Because if this is done right, this is the opportunity to be successful. That's measured in a number of different ways, including making money. And that will drive everything. Investments that restore our economy to one that makes and builds things will create real wealth and drive prosperity for businesses and individuals, while generating more tax revenue."

"I think this is what works," he explains. "It should work everywhere so you don't have a distorted system that eventually implodes because anything that gets too far out of balance eventually loses stability and crashes. We've only seen that a couple of trillion times in history. I'm suggesting a different vision. It's one that's optimistic, that believes anything can be done. It believes that if you say it can't be done, you should get out of the way of those doing it. It believes in human ingenuity and inventiveness, in people's ability to want to do better tomorrow—and the natural inclination for continual improvement. All of that gets lost if you don't have a system that's balanced and supportive."

But DiMicco is quick to distinguish a "can-do attitude of solving problems" from blind optimism that everything will work out fine. As DiMicco sees it, from his perspective as an engineer and his experience as a business leader, we've got to sit down, identify the problem, and devise solutions—as any good engineer or leader would—then implement those solutions efficiently and effectively.

"We don't run from our problems or kick them down the road," DiMicco says. "We face them forthrightly and logically, and refuse to listen to naysayers about what we supposedly can 'never' do."

ONE

THE ECONOMIC CRISIS AND MISSED OPPORTUNITIES

A GOOD LEADER DEALS WITH THE CRISIS HE'S presented, not the one he wants to solve. The first rule of problem solving is to define the problem correctly. Get that part wrong and you're sunk. That's just the way the world works.

If the scale of the economic crisis facing the United States today could be summed up in one number, it wouldn't be $483 billion (the 2014 federal budget deficit) or $17.9 trillion (the national debt as of October 2014) or even $41.8 trillion (Medicare's reported unfunded liability).

The number we need to focus on first and foremost is 30 million. That's the number of jobs I believe the country needs to create by 2025 in order to close the federal government's budget deficit and begin reducing the nation's unfunded entitlement liabilities.

As of September 2014, according to the Bureau of Labor Statistics, total employment had finally returned to its 2007 peak. But in those nearly seven years, the American working population has increased by more than 15 million people. Over 6 million people who would very much like to work are out of the labor force altogether.[1]

On August 1, 2009, when unemployment was still rising and the prospects of economic recovery remained very much in doubt, I sat face-to-face with the president of the United States and told him how to do his job. Respectfully, of course.

The president had invited me, along with three other CEOs representing some of the largest employers in America, to discuss the economic crisis. Howard Schultz of Starbucks was there. So were Walmart's Mike Duke and Verizon's Ivan Seidenberg. Combined, our four companies employ more than 2.5 million Americans. Valerie Jarrett, President Obama's most senior and closest adviser, was also in the room.

To be honest, I was surprised to get the call from the White House. I'd been a pretty vocal critic of President Obama, even before he took the oath of office. I didn't see any point in sugarcoating things now. The president needed to make up a lot of lost ground, in my opinion, and stay clear of any distractions.

For whatever reason that day, the president and some of my fellow CEOs wanted to talk about health care and capping carbon dioxide emissions. Here we were, in the middle of an unprecedented economic crisis, and we were addressing the problems at the margins, like it was just another item on a list. I didn't get it.

Please don't misunderstand me. Health care and climate change are important in their own way. But those topics should have been on the back burner until the real crisis was under control.

Most everyone remembers Rahm Emanuel, Obama's first chief of staff and now the mayor of Chicago, who said, "You never want a serious crisis to go to waste" because "it's an opportunity to do things you didn't think you could do before."[2] That would have been pretty good advice. Too bad the president didn't take it. At the end of the day, the president decides what's the most important thing to be working on. And, I'm sorry, but health care wasn't it.

So I said, "With all due respect, Mr. President, the crisis you have at hand is the one you have to deal with. That crisis is jobs and the economy. Everything else has got to take a backseat. You need to focus on this."

"If you don't handle this crisis," I said, "you won't be remembered for health care or anything else. You'll be remembered as the president who failed to deal with the crisis at hand, and that's the economy and job creation." I still believe that.

As an engineer, I learned early on—and as a corporate leader, I learned a long time ago—if you don't deal with the problem presented to you, then you are by definition a failure. In my experience, everyone comes into a new leadership position with a game plan. But inevitably the real world comes in and ruins it.

Hardly anyone remembers that George W. Bush spent the first nine months of his presidency talking about faith-based initiatives, tax cuts, and education reform. When the country was attacked on September 11, 2001, whatever other grand plans he may have had were set aside.

Bush wanted to fix immigration and Social Security, too, remember? Reality changed the agenda.

Whether or not you liked Bush or agreed with how he responded to 9/11 or the wars in Afghanistan and Iraq, he had his work cut out for him the moment the first plane hit the Twin Towers. Whenever Bush took his eye off the ball and strayed from the crisis, he got into trouble.

The same is true in business. Every time I've taken on a new leadership position, I've faced a crisis I needed to address right away. How you handle that kind of urgency sets you up for success or failure in the eyes of all those around you, whether it's your team in a melt shop in Utah, or a plant with 800 people in Arkansas, or the C-suite at a multi-billion-dollar corporation.

How you handle crisis speaks volumes about you, your leadership style, and your ability to get things done and deal with difficult issues in a way that brings people together as opposed to tearing them apart.

I told the president all of that in 2009. He sat there nodding his head. I know he heard me, but I don't think he was really listening. In any case, his subsequent actions suggest he disregarded everything I had to say.

As a leader, you can't do that.

Now, a good leader also admits when he's wrong. I warned the president that if he didn't tackle the crisis head on, he likely wouldn't have a second term. Obviously, my prediction was way off.

But a leader learns from his mistakes. And the problem Obama avoided confronting directly, or tried to address only with half measures, during his first term is plaguing him in his second. Voters gave

President Obama four more years to get the job done, and done right. He still hasn't acted. He still has time.

UNDERSTANDING THE NUMBERS THAT MATTER

U.S. political leaders think too small when they talk about solving the jobs crisis. All you have to do is compare past recessions with the current economy to understand how lackluster this latest "recovery" has been.

In the 1990s, the economy added an average of 321,000 jobs a month during the best years. The United States added an average of 208,000 jobs a month before the 2008 crash. Now people are cheering over 150,000 jobs a month. In 2013, the economy added just 194,250 jobs a month on average.[3] At that pace, it would take more than eight years to return to the peak employment level the United States enjoyed in 2007, taking into account the millions of Americans entering the workforce. That also assumes the United States won't experience another downturn during that time.

Also, it's important to understand that the government's official unemployment figures often don't tell the whole story.

Every month, the U.S. Department of Labor's Bureau of Labor Statistics releases a jobs report that includes the "official" unemployment rate. It's supposed to measure the percentage of unemployed Americans who have actively looked for work in the previous month. It's a favorite statistic among politicians and journalists. As of September 2014, official unemployment was 5.9 percent.[4]

A month before the November 2012 election, the government reported that official unemployment for September was 7.8 percent. That was the first time since Obama had taken office that the number dropped below 8 percent. Former General Electric CEO Jack Welch caused something of a media firestorm with his response on Twitter: "Unbelievable jobs numbers . . . these Chicago guys will do anything . . . can't debate so change numbers."[5] The night before, Welch wrote, "Tomorrow unemployment numbers for Sept. with all the assumptions Labor Department can make . . . wonder about participation assumption??"[6]

Welch took to the opinion pages of the *Wall Street Journal* to defend himself and elaborate. He pointed out that "official" unemployment doesn't take into account the falling labor participation rate. (See Figure 1.1.) The government doesn't consider the millions of Americans

FIGURE 1.1 AMERICANS LEAVING THE LABOR FORCE

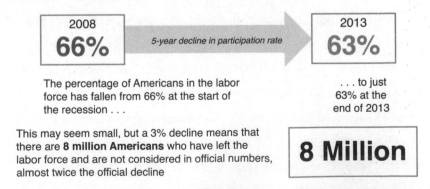

Source: *Bureau of Labor Statistics, Current Population Survey, http://www.bls.gov /cps/.*

who have stopped looking for work to be officially unemployed. Somebody who's been out of work for six months or more who gives up the hunt and no longer claims unemployment benefits *does not count* in the official unemployment tally.

The fact is, almost the entire decline we've seen in "official" unemployment since the recession ended can be explained by all of those Americans who have dropped out of the workforce, as opposed to people finding jobs. Some of them are retirees, but a great many are able-bodied people in the prime of their working lives. And about 7.1 million are working part time when they would rather be working full time—what the government calls "involuntary part-time" workers.

Another fact: in no other economic recovery since 1980 has labor participation *dropped*. Labor participation is supposed to go up during the good times. Not this time.

In his *Wall Street Journal* op-ed, Welch also made some points about all of the flawed ways the government tabulates its unemployment statistics. But he didn't answer the big question: If "official" unemployment is such an unreliable number, then what's the "real" unemployment rate?

At the beginning of 2009, when companies were laying off hundreds of thousands of people every month, real unemployment was 14.2 percent.[7] That includes all of those "involuntary" part-time workers, plus 2.5 million people who have stopped looking for work. Real unemployment peaked at 17.1 percent in October 2009 and remained more or less stuck there for the next year. At the end of 2013, three years into "recovery," real unemployment was 13.1 percent.[8]

FIGURE 1.2   PATH TO 30 MILLION JOBS

Bringing the country back to full employment means creating:

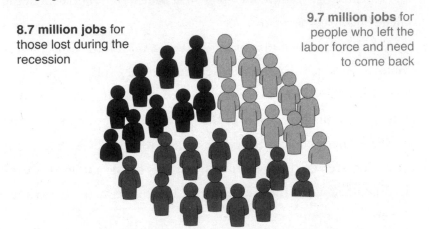

8.7 million jobs for those lost during the recession

9.7 million jobs for people who left the labor force and need to come back

11.6 million jobs for new workers entering the labor force

This means creating **30 million jobs** between now and 2025

Source: *Bureau of Labor Statistics, Current Population Survey, http://www.bls.gov /cps/; Proprietary Analysis by Garten Rothkopf.*

As the graph above shows, we need to create 30 million jobs by 2025 not only to put people currently unemployed back to work, but also to add 1.4 million jobs every year just to keep pace with our population growth.

The goal can't be to create 4 or 5 million new jobs and claim we're back to where we were prior to the crisis. We can't settle for 1 or 2 percent growth every year and call it recovery. We need to be much more ambitious than that.

Some political leaders and economists point to recent improvements in the unemployment rate and say, "See! We're making progress.

FIGURE 1.3   THE REAL UNEMPLOYMENT RATE

The unemployment rate we read about in the papers only considers those actively seeking a job in the last month and ignores nearly **10 million** Americans who need full-time work

20.5 Million

With 20.5 million Americans unemployed or underemployed, the **real rate is 13.1%,** not 6.7%

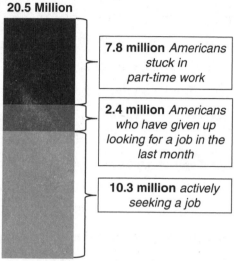

7.8 million *Americans stuck in part-time work*

2.4 million *Americans who have given up looking for a job in the last month*

10.3 million *actively seeking a job*

Source: *Bureau of Labor Statistics, Current Population Survey, http://www.bls.gov /cps/.*

We're recovering." But right now, we can't even produce enough jobs to cover those who are coming into the workforce.

Unemployment may not appear as bad as it was at the bottom of the recession, but it's still much worse than when the crisis began. The U.S. economic engine of job creation is not working anywhere close to capacity, and millions of middle-class families have lost income, benefits, and security, which continues to dampen the recovery.

There are still an awful lot of underutilized people out there. But even that doesn't quite tell the whole story.

The recession hammered younger workers and older workers especially hard. A kid coming out of school used to have real choices, with multiple career paths. Today his options aren't very inspiring. Anyone who graduated from college in the past four or five years has found it next to impossible to get a well-paying job geared to his skills.

More than half of young college-aged adults are either jobless or underemployed, more than at any time in 11 years. Today, millions of college graduates live at home, often saddled with huge student loan debt.

I read a survey recently that showed an incredible 85 percent of recent college grads said they planned to move back in with their parents. Maybe they're saving on rent, or maybe they're playing around on Twitter and Facebook all day. In any case, instead of building or making something useful, millions of college graduates are slinging hash or selling Chinese-made tennis shoes someplace. What a waste of young, energetic talent!

The longer a college graduate is out of work, the worse her career prospects look over time. After just six months of unemployment, a 23-year-old with a bachelor degree can expect to earn 7 percent less than her peers on average by the time she reaches her fortieth birthday. And because the cost of college tuition has increased twelvefold in the past 30 years, she'll have massive loans to repay and fewer options to repay them.

At the other end of the spectrum, a couple of very unhealthy trends have taken hold among older workers. First, workers nearing the end of their careers—people in their 50s or early 60s—who lose their jobs

FIGURE 1.4   YOUTH UNEMPLOYMENT AND STUDENT DEBT

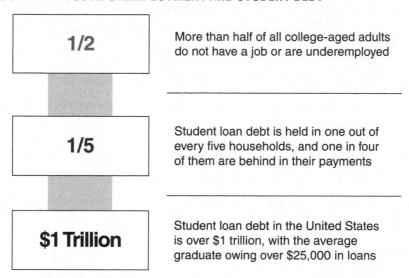

1/2	More than half of all college-aged adults do not have a job or are underemployed
1/5	Student loan debt is held in one out of every five households, and one in four of them are behind in their payments
$1 Trillion	Student loan debt in the United States is over $1 trillion, with the average graduate owing over $25,000 in loans

Source: *Richard Fry, "A Record One-in-Five Households Now Owe Student Loan Debt," Pew Research, September 26, 2012, http://www.pewsocialtrends. org/2012/09/26/a-record-one-in-five-households-now-owe-student-loan-debt/; "Federal Survey of Consumer Finances," Board of Governors of the Federal System, http://www.federalreserve.gov/econresdata/scf/scfindex.htm; "Regional Economic Press Briefing," Federal Reserve Bank of New York, June 27, 2013, http://www.newyorkfed .org/newsevents/mediaadvisory/2013/Presentations_06272013.pdf.*

are much less likely to return to the workforce the longer they're out of work. The longer anyone is out of work—six months, nine months, or a year—the harder it is to land a new job. But it's especially tough for older workers, who usually commanded higher salaries before they were laid off.

I hear that a lot of employers look at older workers as overqualified for most jobs, when in fact they're perfectly qualified. They have skills, knowledge, and decades of experience. In this economy, who wouldn't want that?

Imagine a 59-year-old cabinetmaker that got laid off three years ago when his company closed its factory in Ohio and moved operations to Vietnam. He made enough money to buy a nice house for his family, and maybe a couple of cars. He could afford to put his son through college, but he lost his job just as his daughter graduated from high school. So his daughter has taken out $30,000 in loans to go to school. Meanwhile, he's making minimum wage at a temp agency and doing odd jobs where he can find them.

That man's skills are going to waste, and his middle-class lifestyle has disappeared. And his odds of finding another job like the one he lost aren't good, but at least he's working part time. If his 62-year-old neighbor lost her job around the same time and didn't find another job within 17 months, her chances of finding another job in the next three months would be roughly 6 percent.[9]

Now what is that lady supposed to do? She might try to collect unemployment for a while and keep looking for work. Or she could apply for Social Security three years early. She wouldn't be the first. The federal government says four in ten workers who lost their jobs in the recession did just that. The downside, of course, is that her monthly benefit would be cut between 20 and 30 percent. And, no, it won't go up on her sixty-fifth birthday. She'll have to live with drastically reduced benefits for the rest of her life.

Lest we forget, the stock market crash and recession hurt millions of people who staked their retirements on Wall Street's success. Many older workers who managed to keep their jobs during the downturn lost their 401(k) savings. They're working longer to rebuild some of the savings they lost, deferring or postponing retirement as long as they can—and crowding out younger workers. It's madness.

WHERE THE JOBS ARE—
AND WHERE WE REALLY NEED THEM

It's a scandal that so many of our people aren't working, but it isn't a surprise. The reason boils down to the fact that almost all the jobs that were created over the past couple of decades were in fictitious "service businesses." Those jobs are gone.

Just as we need to understand who was hurt most by the economic crisis, we also need a clear idea of where most of the jobs were lost— and where we need most of the new jobs. The two aren't necessarily the same. But if we're going to resolve this crisis and create 30 million jobs, we need more Americans building, making, and innovating things, and fewer people working in low-paying service jobs.

Construction and manufacturing accounted for half of the 8 million jobs lost between 2008 and 2010. Parts of the manufacturing sector—the automotive industry in particular—have recovered somewhat since 2010. But recent gains are tiny compared to long-term losses. In the meantime, service industry jobs, which declined 5 percent during the same period, have returned to prerecession levels and continue to grow.[10]

According to the Bureau of Labor Statistics, the fastest-growing occupations in the next five years will all be in service-oriented businesses, including things like health-care support staff, customer service, and food preparation. None of those jobs require a college degree, but the bigger problem is that very few of them pay well.

We really shouldn't be aching for more service-sector work. In practice, it means a North Carolina textile worker who a few years ago made $15 an hour sewing blankets at a mill is now making $10 an hour as a cook at a county jail. We see stories like that all the time. I mention textiles in particular because as recently as a decade ago it was one of the largest manufacturing employers in the state. But North Carolina apparel makers have been destroyed by cheap foreign imports. The United States has lost nearly a million textile jobs since 1999. Why do we put up with this?

Construction and manufacturing are the sectors where the economy is bleeding jobs and where we have the greatest need. Problem Solving 101 says if we want to turn this crisis around, we need to figure out what is preventing those sectors from growing and then address those factors. We shouldn't spend a lot of time and money trying to retrain skilled construction and manufacturing workers and move them into low-skill, low-wage service "careers."

Understand, I have nothing against home health-care aides, line cooks, or customer service reps. But those jobs *cannot* sustain a middle class, which has been shrinking since the 1970s. We need more electricians, machinists, welders, and engineers—for starters. Any lasting solution to our crisis needs to focus on putting people back to work in jobs that create tangible wealth and allowing the U.S. economy and the American middle class to grow. If we simply create 30 million low-wage service jobs that don't provide families a decent, middle-class lifestyle, we haven't solved the problem.

HOW OUR POLITICAL LEADERSHIP KEEPS GETTING THE PROBLEM WRONG

America's political leadership right now isn't rising to the challenge, which is unlike any other economic crisis the country has ever seen. Republicans and Democrats are either caught up in trivial pursuits, or they're failing to take the problem seriously. It's a bipartisan catastrophe.

Trying to solve our jobs crisis with billion-dollar home weatherization programs (which was part of the $787 billion stimulus) and other trendy green subsidies told me right away that the Democrats didn't understand the scale of the problem. They did not define the problem correctly, so they were doomed to fail from the start.

Republicans in Congress don't fully understand the crisis, either. If they did, they wouldn't be so obsessed with the national debt. Yes, the $17.9 trillion debt is a problem, especially if left unchecked. But Republicans never should have let the debt blind them to the larger crisis.

What's missing here is real leadership. Good leaders put their agenda aside to deal with a crisis of this magnitude. The trouble is, Republicans and Democrats alike have tried to redefine the economic crisis to fit the policies they really want, rather than address the crisis for what it really is. One party is talking about one-tenth of the solution; the other party is talking about another tenth; and each side is rejecting the best of what the other side has to offer out of pure political calculation. Most of their answers have been too small, too unambitious—and too partisan. Republicans keep beating the drum for tax cuts, while Democrats keep beating the drum for higher tax rates, as if overhauling the tax code will solve all of our problems.

Republicans used to understand the importance of investing in the nation's infrastructure. By obsessing over the debt, they've missed countless chances to advance policies that would turn the economy around and make long-term debt reduction much less painful.

Shortly after my meeting with the president in August 2009, I attended another Washington luncheon with a group of CEOs and 35 Democratic senators, including Max Baucus, Chuck Schumer, Dianne Feinstein, Dick Durbin, and Senate Majority Leader Harry Reid. Once again, the topic was the economic crisis and how to get joblessness under control. The *real* unemployment rate would plateau at 17.1 percent in October of that year and remain there—with a brief dip the following January—until April 2010.

When my turn came to speak, I repeated the same message I'd been delivering for years. Only then had it begun to break through. I told them, "Look, the true dimension of the crisis is that for 30 years we've supported a failed business model for our economy that said we could ignore being a nation that creates, makes, and builds things; that we could remain a rich nation that only services things." We went out of our way to dismantle what made this country great, while other countries around the world are building their way to greatness. And we focused on a phony wealth creation model that created bubble after bubble and ruined millions of middle-class families.

As I told these senators, settling for meager growth and adding 100,000 service jobs a month won't save us. We need a national strategy to start creating 200,000 or 300,000 jobs a month over the next five years.

To his great credit, Schumer stood up and said, "He's got it. He's right. This is what we need to do." Feinstein agreed with me, too. That same month in 2009, Toyota Motor Corporation announced it would close the Fremont, California factory the company had operated since 1984 with General Motors. The decision would cost at least 4,700 union jobs, most of which would go back to Japan. Feinstein later confessed that Toyota's departure made her realize just how much government policy can hurt industry. "We actually drove Toyota out of California," she said. "They left California, and it was our regulations that drove them out."

But in a roomful of big egos, not everyone was going to be so easily persuaded to part with long-held assumptions. I shouldn't have been surprised when a prominent Democrat stood up and said, "Are you telling me we've got to stop everything we're doing and change direction?" And I said, "Yeah, that's what leaders do when there's a crisis that requires it."

Then another senator, a Democrat from a Great Lakes state, piped up with his own solution. He said—I'm paraphrasing a little bit here— we've got to start taking these kids coming out of college and putting them to work in our national parks. And we need to do it in time for the next election.

I listened to this senator's monologue, thinking to myself, *Somebody spends tens—no, hundreds of thousands of dollars sending their kid to four years of college, just so they can go work in a park picking up garbage? No way!*

I said, "Excuse me, senator. If you are trying to create jobs in time for next November's election, you're going to fail. If you try to create real jobs for the next five years, you'll be successful."

But he would hear none of it. He was interested only in getting quick numbers with make-work jobs at national parks, or putting college grads to work recaulking windows in old buildings. Like so many other politicians, he just wanted to use the crisis as an excuse to redefine the policies he's pushed for years and ensure his reelection.

The partisanship and rancor has only gotten worse inside the Beltway. Three years later, I found myself sitting once again in a meeting with this same group of Democratic congressional leaders. And once again, the topic was jobs, with a special emphasis on infrastructure. I reminded everyone what I said in 2009, and asked point-blank how they could ignore the economic crisis in front of them.

At that point, Senator John Kerry interrupted me and said I should save my breath for the Republicans, who refused to cooperate or compromise. Now, I'm not saying the Republicans haven't shirked responsibility; both parties share blame for the state of our job market and economy. But don't forget, the Democrats squandered a big opportunity to address the deeply dysfunctional economy in the first two years of Obama's administration. So I took another breath and told Senator Kerry, "Just one problem with that. Before 2010, you had the presidency, you had the House, and you had a filibuster-proof majority in the Senate. It's a shame you weren't able to get anything done. Now you can't blame the Republicans."

SOME LESSONS LEARNED

When Democratic or Republican leaders talk about the economy, they use the wrong frames of reference and the wrong metrics to measure success. The Obama administration claimed credit for creating 4 million jobs but never addressed the need for policies that would empower America's businesses and entrepreneurs to create *seven times* that number. And they played down the inconvenient fact that those new jobs lagged well behind the number of new entrants into the U.S. workforce.

That might be good politics. But it's shameful leadership.

What I took from those meetings with the president and congressional leaders was this: If you are a national politician who wants to get reelected, you don't talk about a real unemployment rate of 14 or 15 percent. Instead, you tout how "official" unemployment is falling. You fixate on small solutions with unproven or overhyped benefits, such as green jobs. You give lip service to big solutions that would actually put millions of Americans to work, like developing shale oil and natural gas, and investing in the nation's crumbling infrastructure, while voting against vital spending and approving new rules to stop new energy development in its tracks.

I've learned over the years to pay less attention to what a politician says in a campaign speech and keep a close eye on his actions. Deeds— actual policies—matter far more than words.

So, for example, President Obama has repeatedly called for the doubling of U.S. exports. He's right! That's essential. But how do we expect to be successful if we can't compete in our own market because of growth-impeding policies at home and massive trade-distorting policies of our competitors overseas? We can't. So the choice is clear: correct the problem, or watch the middle class keep sliding downward.

I worry because even after the 2012 election, the country is as polarized as ever. Look at the fight over the fiscal cliff. Look at the sequester. Look at the government shutdown. Those crises were totally unnecessary. President Obama and Congress are sowing more divisiveness instead of bringing Americans together. Obama's failure to understand his unique role has fostered an environment that is stunting what otherwise could be very strong growth in job creation and in our economy. The president can't keep punting the problem. Failing to fix the jobs crisis within the next few years will have long-lasting implications.

Annual growth of gross domestic product is hardly the last word on the health of America's economy—especially given the decline in wages middle-income Americans have experienced even during robust periods of expansion. But GDP is useful in thinking about what's been lost and what could be gained. The difference between settling for a meager 2 percent GDP growth over the next ten years and striving for 4 percent growth is $3 trillion.

Would you leave that kind of money sitting on the table? Of course you wouldn't. Think about that! Think about the squandered opportunity and lost productivity. Not to mention the lost tax revenue.

Our leaders in the White House and in Congress haven't taken any meaningful steps to spur the kind of economic revival we need or to ensure we have a strong and thriving middle class again in this country. We can choose growth, or we can choose to follow countries like Greece, Italy, and Spain down the path of cronyism, stagnation, and unchecked debt. Any question about which path we're on now?

It's a mistake to look at the current crisis from the standpoint of a couple of election cycles. We didn't get here yesterday. Truth is, we've done nothing to correct 30 years of slipshod economics or 20 years of failed, unbalanced trade policies. In order to understand how those policies came about, we need a broader historical perspective.

TWO

NO MORE MOONSHOTS

*(Or, How the United States Won the
Space Race and Stopped Racing)*

"IF WE COULD PUT A MAN ON THE MOON . . ." IT
may be a cliché, but it's a useful one for looking at how the United States
got into the current crisis, and for understanding what we need to do
to get out of it.

Just as the current crisis didn't suddenly materialize when Lehman
Brothers went belly up in 2008, the entire United States of America
didn't wake up one morning and decide we wouldn't go back to the
moon or send astronauts to Mars. But without question, the United
States moved away from being the country that beat the Soviet Union
to the moon 45 years ago to a country that talks about maybe sending

manned missions to the moon and Mars at some vague point in the future. What happened?

Very simply, priorities shifted, and some very bad ideas took hold. Bureaucracies expanded and laws changed. The culture changed, too. But all of that took time.

When I was a child in Mount Kisco, New York, for the longest time I dreamed of building rockets for NASA. As someone who came of age during the space race, I certainly wasn't the only kid with that dream. I was 11 when John F. Kennedy went to Congress in May 1961 and announced that putting a man on the moon should be at the top of the nation's list of priorities. Kennedy renewed the call the next year at Houston's Rice University, in what would become one of his more memorable speeches. Kennedy spoke not far from where NASA would run the 1969 mission that secured Neil Armstrong's place in history.

For me—and for millions of young Americans in the early 1960s— Kennedy's words were inspiration to pursue a career in science and engineering. That speech also reflected the optimism of the era and offered a reminder of what a nation could do with the right kind of leadership, the right policies, and the right kind of partnership between the public and private sectors.

"No nation which expects to be the leader of other nations can expect to stay behind in the race for space," Kennedy told a stadium full of students and dignitaries on September 12, 1962. "For the eyes of the world now look into space, to the moon and to the planets beyond, and we have vowed that we shall not see it governed by a hostile flag of conquest, but by a banner of freedom and peace. But it will be done. And it will be done before the end of this decade."[1]

The Cold War was in its most dangerous years. America was prosperous and growing, but we lived under the fear of another world war and the threat of nuclear annihilation. The Soviet Union had launched Sputnik on October 4, 1957, and it was a wake-up call. President Dwight Eisenhower called it the "Sputnik crisis." The United States was badly lagging the Soviets in the space race, and Americans understood right away that if the Russians could fire a rocket that delivered a satellite into space, they could easily fire a rocket to deliver a nuclear weapon anywhere.

Americans came together to meet the Sputnik crisis head-on, passing the National Defense Education Act to pump millions of dollars into science and math programs in public schools, and investing additional millions in the U.S. space program.

But that wasn't enough. America got a second wake-up call in 1961, when the Russians sent Yuri Gagarin into space, another Soviet first. We answered by launching Alan Shepard into low earth orbit, followed by John Glenn's trip into outer space a year later. Kennedy knew we had to do better. If we were going to beat the Russians in the space race, we needed to innovate and develop new technology to put an American on the moon first.

"We choose to go to the moon," Kennedy said. "We choose to go to the moon in this decade and do the other things, not because they are easy, but because they are hard, because that goal will serve to organize and measure the best of our energies and skills, because that challenge is one that we are willing to accept, one we are unwilling to postpone, and one which we intend to win, and the others, too."[2]

Kennedy also knew he couldn't just talk about going to the moon. This couldn't be an empty motivational speech, forgotten the next week.

The country would need to spend money. Billions of dollars. He warned up front that spending those billions offered no clear or guaranteed return on investment. "I realize that this is in some measure an act of faith and vision," Kennedy said, "for we do not now know what benefits await us." He added, "I don't think we ought to waste any money, but I think we ought to do the job."[3]

When it was over, the United States had spent nearly $30 billion on the Apollo program, the equivalent of $202 billion today. I'd submit very few people would say that was money badly spent.

What's most interesting to me about the Apollo program is that it was a response to a threat, wrapped in a vision for a better tomorrow, presented by a great communicator that people wanted to support. That's leadership. And it was all done in partnership with the private sector.

I'm a big believer in public-private partnerships, but I know there is a lot of skepticism about them. People point to cases of waste, fraud, and abuse and say public-private partnerships don't work, that they're bad for the taxpayer. Not true. The United States has done great things when the public sector and the private sector work together, from winning a world war to winning the space race.

After all, who built the Saturn and Gemini rockets that sent the Apollo crews into space and onto the lunar surface? NASA didn't run rocket factories. It was companies like Bell Labs, Boeing, General Electric, and Rocketdyne, working in partnership with the government, that made Apollo such a great success.

Academics and economists apparently can't come to a consensus on what actually constitutes a public-private partnership. It's really not so hard. When you bring the whole country together to deal with a problem—it could be a threat to national security, or it could be the worst economic crisis since the Depression—you can deal with anything. That, in my view, is a public-private partnership in its very best sense.

Another way to understand public-private partnerships is the relationship between elected officials and voters. Taxpayers elect people to office and pay their salaries to do certain things. One is to ensure their money is well spent. But the greatest of those is to keep the country together, able to work for mutual prosperity and the public good.

Forging a successful public-private partnership requires sound leadership—the type of leadership Eisenhower and Kennedy displayed in the face of Soviet advances, and the type Ronald Reagan would later bring to the negotiating table not only with the Russians, but also the Germans and the Japanese when America's balance of trade depended on it. We're missing that kind of leadership right now. We shouldn't be electing leaders to divide and conquer. That's the opposite of a good public-private partnership. But that's the mode they're in right now, and they have been for quite some time. I say that's a failure of leadership because we're always going to have warring tribes, so to speak. But if you they have the ear of both those warring tribes, you can get them all to pull in the same direction.

It takes salesmanship; it takes passion; it takes a message that makes sense to everybody and a common thread that everybody can support, even if they may not like each other. Our nation's problems are much bigger than ourselves. But our leaders haven't gotten the message. They're dividing society—rich versus poor, men versus women, black versus white—when they should be bringing us together.

INSPIRING A GENERATION: "WE MEAN TO LEAD"

Why did America put men on the moon? Kennedy couldn't have been clearer: "No nation which expects to be the leader of other nations can expect to stay behind in the race for space. We mean to be a part of it—we mean to lead it." No ambiguity there.

Kennedy's speech inspired the country and a whole generation. Science education in the United States really peaked during that time, because the country made it a priority.

By the time I got to high school in the mid-1960s, Kennedy was gone, but the United States was well on its way to reaching his goal. Within four years of his moon speech, Congress had quadrupled the nation's space exploration budget.

It was great time for any kid with an aptitude for math and science, like me. I felt lucky, and I had options. Engineering was a natural fit for me. My parents thought engineering would provide a good living, so they urged me on in my studies. I heard the same message from my school guidance counselors. It wasn't always easy. But I enjoyed the subjects, worked hard, and did well enough to be accepted to Brown University.

I had originally planned to major in electrical engineering. Boy, what a rude awakening that was. I went from earning straight As in high school to flunking my very first exam in an introductory engineering class. I scored 30 out of 100. Later I found out that the top score was a 50, and the professor graded on a curve—thank God! But it still wasn't great. I really struggled my freshman year at Brown. I sought out Barrett Hazeltine, one of the associate deans. Hazeltine was a good guy, very student-oriented and well liked. He was willing to tutor me. In fact, he mentored thousands of undergraduates over his 50-year career. He still teaches a couple of courses on entrepreneurship and technology at Brown every year.

I eventually got into the electrical engineering program, but I wasn't happy. I remember sitting in one of those big stadiumlike classrooms, listening to this professor lecture and write on a stacked blackboard. He would talk and write, write and talk. As soon as he filled a board, he'd push it up and begin writing on the one underneath. And so on. For 40 minutes. Every class. Well, if that was what the next four years had in store, forget it. I wasn't going to make it as an electrical engineer. But I still wanted to study engineering. I switched to metallurgy and materials science, because I figured NASA would need people who understood alloys, stresses, and heat as much as they needed electrical engineers.

I graduated from college just as the Apollo program was winding down. But happily, NASA was developing a space station—Skylab— and the space shuttle program was well underway. I interviewed with General Electric at its uranium enrichment facility in Wilmington, North Carolina, and in Massachusetts, where the company did its research and development work.

But truth be told, I felt like I didn't know enough when I got my bachelor's degree. Graduate school seemed like the way to go. I applied to business schools and engineering schools, and got accepted into several of both, including Brown's engineering school and the University of Pennsylvania. I loved Brown, and I really liked my professors there. But everyone told me I should go to a different grad school than where I went to college. That sounded reasonable enough.

Choosing a grad school involved some practical decision making too. All of the business schools said they'd be happy to loan me $5,000 a year. The engineering schools said they'd be happy to pay for my books and tuition, and they'd throw in $5,000 a year as a stipend. Well, that was an easy decision. My family wasn't rich. I had three younger sisters and a brother at home, and my mother and father both worked. Dad owned a soda and beer distributorship with my uncle in Mount Kisco. I was cleaning bathrooms to make a little extra money.

I earned my master's degree in engineering at the University of Pennsylvania. In the meantime, I married the love of my life. But by the time I finished up my graduate work and started looking for a job, NASA wasn't hiring. One of my professors at UPenn had done a lot of work in the steel industry—the very industry my engineering buddies said we would never, ever work in. But he knew some people at Republic Steel's R&D lab in Cleveland, and they needed bright young guys. So even though I'd never studied steel for my master's degree, all of a sudden I was in the steel business. You just never know how things are going to work out.

From the day I entered high school in New York to the moment I left graduate school in Pennsylvania, the United States had worked toward one of its greatest triumphs while turning a blind eye to the bad effects of some old policies. The late 1960s and early 1970s saw an economic upheaval that was set in motion by the end of World War II. At the same time, just as Americans began to reap real benefits from exploring the moon, the country seemed to lose interest and give up.

We went from being a nation that put a man on the moon to one that can't seem to do it again. We won a world war, built a state-of-the-art interstate highway system, and rebuilt Japan and Europe. Now, the president of the United States and Congress are talking about slashing national defense spending, our national highways are crumbling, and another visit to the moon is years, if not decades, away.

How did we get from *there* to *here?* I'd say the short answer is, we got complacent, and our leaders lost sight of what's important.

The United States gradually ceded manned space exploration to our competitors, just as, over time, we abandoned manufacturing and embraced service-oriented industries in the name of "free trade." That's something you should never, ever do. I know I say you should never say "never," but this is an exception that really only proves the rule.

In 50 years of doing business, Nucor never abandoned the low-end steel markets the way the big, integrated steel producers did. We still make joists and rebar after all these years, but we also make high-end products—beams and pilings, hot-rolled sheet, you name it. We figured out how to leverage technology to be profitable at both the low *and* high ends of the market. Too many big corporations abandon markets to their competitors because they're too slow and too bureaucratic to remain competitive. That's why the Bethlehems and Republics are out of business and Nucor is still going strong.

As with companies, so it is with countries. The last American space shuttle flight was in 2011. Our shuttles are now museum pieces. If a U.S. astronaut needs to visit the International Space Station, he has to hitch an expensive ride on a Russian shuttle.

In 2010, President Obama talked about America's future in space. He had just cut $81 billion in funding for NASA's Constellation program, ending the program that was supposed to return Americans to the moon as early as 2020 to begin a building a permanent base there. Many critics said Constellation was too expensive. President Obama promised $6 billion in additional funding for NASA over the next five years. He also said the United States would return to the moon and Americans would set foot on Mars someday.

But unlike President Kennedy 50 years earlier, Obama set no deadline. He provided no urgency to act. As we're talking about maybe going back to the moon someday, China is building its manned space program with the same energy and determination that we built ours in the 1960s. Did you know the Chinese plan to have a man on the moon within the next decade, maybe as early as 2020? We've fallen way behind.

Of course, we can put a man on the moon again! But we have a lot of catch-up work to do first.

At some point, serious distortions took hold in U.S. policy and economics. To locate when and how those distortions came about, we look to America's emergence as a global superpower. Shortsighted policy making after World War II took U.S. economic supremacy for granted and bred the dangerous complacency that moved us away from being a country that creates, builds, and makes things—a country that could put a man on the moon—to one that thinks we can make something from nothing . . . hence, bubble after bubble after bubble.

THREE

DISTORTED TRADE AND THE RISE OF THE FALSE ECONOMY

A GALLUP POLL IN EARLY 2013 FOUND THAT A plurality of Americans believe the country's best days are behind us and expect more economic difficulties ahead.[1] Such persistent pessimism is something new in American life, a marked departure from the optimism that shaped the postwar era. How did that happen?

After the United States won World War II, the American people and their elected leaders undertook one of the most expensive reconstruction projects in its history. The United States was the last great power left standing, with astonishing industrial output—accounting for 40 percent of the total U.S. economy in 1950[2]—and a dynamic market.

Instead of subjugating the Japanese and annexing Germany, and bleeding their treasuries dry, the United States helped rebuild the societies responsible for sending the world headlong into the deadliest war ever witnessed by mankind.

The United States enacted the European Recovery Program, better known as the Marshall Plan, which poured $13 billion in development aid into western Europe (about $117 billion in today's dollars) and, incidentally, helped keep international communism contained. We took a similar approach with Japan, where the Allied powers forgave most of its war debt and provided nearly $2 billion in direct aid and low-interest loans. The United States also stimulated the Japanese economy during the Korean War through the "special procurement" program, in which the Pentagon bought new military equipment from Japan (such as jeeps from Nissan and Toyota) to use on the Korean peninsula.

But at some point in the decades following the war, U.S. companies like Nucor recognized that Japan and Germany were no longer war-torn nations; they were, in fact, formidable industrialized nations competing with us for manufacturing jobs. In the Nixon, Ford, and Carter presidencies, our national leaders were asleep at the switch while German and Japanese manufacturers began taking more and more global market share—and with it, more and more American jobs.

The result was not free trade, as they would have you believe, but *preferential* trade and a distorted economy. The truth is, losing a war isn't the only way for a nation to lose its freedom—it can also be lost by surrendering its economic power. If we aren't careful, our enemies won't even need to fire a shot.

WHEN HELPING HURTS

The United States has always been "a shining city on a hill," and God willing, it always will be. American altruism is remarkable. We fight for freedom and democracy, not for conquest. We want to live as free people and we want others to be free, too. After World War II, that was the goal behind our reconstruction efforts in Germany and Japan.

The landscape in 1945 was brutal. The industrial capacities of Japan, Germany, and most of Europe had been blasted to pieces. The markets overseas were in rubble, and the war's losers were broke, starving, and unsure about the future. We could have made the same mistake the victorious armies did after World War I. We could have saddled our former enemies with crushing war reparations and created the dynamics for another dictator to rise, just as Hitler did after the Kaiser was deposed and the weak Weimar Republic crumbled in the midst of the Depression.

If the Germans and the Japanese were ever to get back to a point where they could create wealth again, they needed someplace to sell. So the United States said, "We'll buy!" In fact, we became their biggest customers.

Now, it wasn't pure altruism. We also had our own practical interests to consider. We wanted to protect the hard-won gains at places like the Battle of the Bulge and Iwo Jima. To prevent the rise of fascism or succumbing to communism, America advanced its interests by spending billions of dollars shoring up a free-market system in Europe and Asia. We decided to be magnanimous. We treated the defeated Germans and Japanese the way we would want to be treated, because the United States wanted a stronger, freer, safer, and more democratic world. The Allies offered the vanquished Axis countries certain advantages in trade and aid because most everyone understood that the world would be a much better place if the Germans and Japanese were building cars and making radios rather than tanks and bombs.

Temporary measures to help war-ravaged nations rebuild made sense. And our aid was necessary—it was absolutely the right thing to do. We could accommodate market-distorting policies for a while. We could even put up with abusive trade policies. Why not? The United States was riding high in the 1950s and the early 1960s. But at some point, we should have told the Japanese and the Germans, "You're on your own."

When suddenly we find the countries that we reduced to rubble in a world war are outpacing our manufacturing base and pummeling our job-creation engine through currency manipulation and state-owned enterprises, then something's got to change.

AN ADULT CONVERSATION

With the arrival of the 1970s, the world trade situation, fostered by policies like the Marshall Plan, was boomeranging back on the United States. Our brand of altruism had gotten out of hand. Policies that might have made sense in 1945, or even 1965, didn't make sense anymore. Japan and West Germany were growing fast, adapting cutting-edge technologies, and exporting everything from cars to copy machines. Americans saw prices go up on everything from bread to gasoline as their wages began to fall. People realized the United

FIGURE 3.1 CHANGES IN GLOBAL MANUFACTURING

During the the 1970s, '80s, and '90s, U.S. share of
global manufacturing stayed nearly constant while
Japan and Germany's increased by 50%

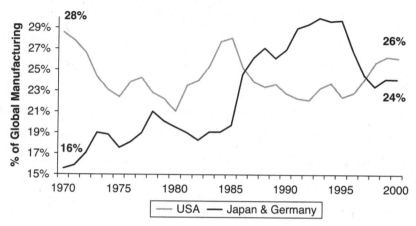

Source: *"GDP by Type of Expenditure and Value Added by Kind of Economic Activity,
Annual, 1970-2012," UN Conference on Trade and Development Statistics, http://
unctadstat.unctad.org/wds/TableViewer/tableView.aspx?ReportId=95.*

States might have defeated Japan and Germany in the war, but we
were losing our economy.

At some point in the 1970s, the American president should have
called a time-out and had that adult conversation with the Germans
and the Japanese. The president needed to say, in no uncertain terms,
we would no longer allow Japan and Germany to abuse our markets by
unfairly depreciating their currencies against our dollar, making their
goods artificially cheaper to import and ours more expensive to export.
We should have insisted on a level playing field.

The analogy I use is a parent and a child. At some point, the kids have to stand on their own two feet. Otherwise, they become dependent and start to think what's theirs is theirs and what's yours is theirs. Obviously, that's a terrible lesson to teach a child.

Sometimes mom and dad have to sit Johnny or Janey down and have a hard talk: "We love you, but it's time for you to go out on your own. If you need somebody to talk to, we're here. But if you try to steal the silverware, you're in trouble."

Richard Nixon didn't have that conversation. Neither did Gerald Ford. Jimmy Carter tried to protect the steel industry through an elaborate "trigger" scheme that set a minimum price for foreign imports, but he didn't enforce the rules very well. Companies found ways to exploit loopholes allowing domestic steel distributors to open a foreign office, buy cheap foreign steel, and sell it in the United States at a higher price. The whole scheme was a bust—it was bad for companies that did the right thing and played by the rules. And as a result of that profound leadership failure, one American business after another fell under the onslaught of industries either owned directly or indirectly by foreign governments—autos, steel, semiconductors, microchips, televisions, radios, cameras, toys, and on and on.

ENTER THE PLAZA ACCORD

At the heart of the Japanese and German trade policies was an effort to devalue their currency. Japan had a large trade deficit in the early 1960s, for example. But by 1971, the Japanese had a trade surplus of $5.8 billion—the equivalent of $33.6 billion in 2014.[3] Even after the

United States took steps to force other countries to revalue their currencies rather than devalue the dollar in the face of rising inflation, the Japanese government responded by intervening extensively in its currency markets, buying and selling dollars to keep the yen's value as low as possible. West Germany did much the same with its deutschmark.

The distorted currency rates favored both countries' manufacturing sectors by making their products cheaper compared to their American competitors. The dollar had appreciated in value immensely in the early 1980s, again partly as a result of the U.S. Federal Reserve's efforts to rein in the inflation and stagflation of the 1970s. The U.S. trade deficit ballooned to nearly 3 percent of the nation's gross domestic product from 1980 to 1985. U.S. exports fell, hitting manufacturers hard. U.S. companies, including General Electric and Caterpillar, lobbied hard for an agreement that would revalue the U.S. currency against the Japanese yen, German mark, and British pound sterling.

The bloodletting went on for 15 years longer than it should have. President Ronald Reagan finally stopped it, at least for a little while, and he did so in a truly bipartisan way. In 1985, he persuaded Congress to pass legislation outlawing foreign currency manipulation. Reagan worked with the Democratic Speaker of the House, Tip O'Neill, and the CEOs of Caterpillar and General Electric to get it done. Reagan and O'Neill didn't see eye-to-eye on much, but they agreed that something had to be done about foreign governments intentionally devaluing their currencies to undermine the American economy. If we didn't act, Reagan and O'Neill both understood, America would go out of business. That was a model of bipartisan leadership, when two individuals with two very different conceptions of the world got together, had a drink or two, and agreed that American manufacturing was worth saving. The free-market fundamentalists didn't like it, and Reagan took some political flak, but it was the right thing to do. Millions of jobs were on the line.

Together they also rallied America's business leaders. Reagan convinced the Business Roundtable and the U.S. Chamber of Commerce that the Japanese and the Germans needed to revalue the yen and the deutschmark. With legislation in hand, he assembled Japanese and German delegations and had his personal trade negotiators gather in the Plaza Hotel in Manhattan in September 1985. Essentially, Reagan pulled the Japanese and Germans into the Plaza and said, in so many words, "All right, how do you want to do this? The easy way or the hard way? You can't manipulate your currency anymore. You either revalue it immediately, or we'll revalue it for you by slapping tariffs on your goods."

The goal was straightforward: a multinational agreement to devalue the U.S. dollar in relation to the Japanese yen and the German mark, with the goal of balancing the U.S. trade deficit and stimulating American exports. The Germans and the Japanese agreed.

After the Plaza Accord, trade rose, and currency manipulation subsided. In just two years, the value of the deutschmark compared to the dollar fell 36 percent,[4] and the value of the Japanese yen fell 39 percent.[5] The U.S. trade deficit improved more than 50 percent in just a few years.[6] U.S. exports to western Europe and Japan increased. Hundreds of Japanese manufacturers, including giants like Toyota and NEC Corporation, would open factories in the United States to take advantage of the cost difference.

FIGURE 3.2   PLAZA ACCORD TRADE IMPACT

The Plaza Accord lowered our trade deficits with Japan and
West Germany

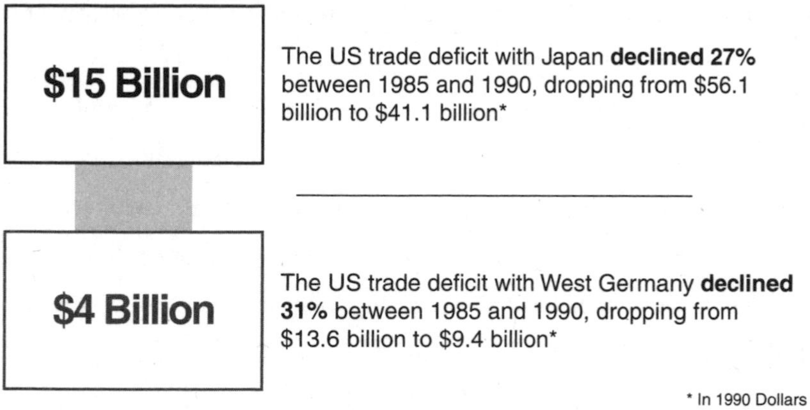

$15 Billion	The US trade deficit with Japan **declined 27%** between 1985 and 1990, dropping from $56.1 billion to $41.1 billion*
$4 Billion	The US trade deficit with West Germany **declined 31%** between 1985 and 1990, dropping from $13.6 billion to $9.4 billion*

* In 1990 Dollars

Source: *"U.S Trade in Goods by Country," U.S. Census Bureau Foreign Trade Data,*
http://www.census.gov/foreign-trade/balance/.

It worked, and it worked darn well. In fact, the Plaza Accord may
have worked *too* well. In 1987, the same parties signed the Louvre Accord to halt the rapid depreciation of the U.S. dollar. Now, there are
those who claim that Japan's so-called lost decade—the period of slow,
stagnant growth between 1991 and 2000, but really covering the period
from 1991 until 2011 or so—was a direct result of the Plaza Accord.
If that's true, when was Germany's lost decade? Of course, they didn't
have one. Unfortunately for the Japanese, they were much more dependent upon the currency manipulation tool than the Germans were.

For companies like Nucor, the Plaza Accord was a necessary cor-
rective and lifeline. U.S. manufacturers, which had been hammered by

inflation and the double-dip recession of the early 1980s, began show-
ing new signs of life. The deal also created conditions that led directly
to a fruitful partnership between Nucor and Japan's Yamato Kogyo
Company—a partnership that had a profound effect on the trajectory
of the company and my career.

It just so happened that in the year after the Plaza Accord, Nucor
was looking for ways to expand into bigger, higher-value markets. We
were never afraid of expanding when expansion made sense. When I
started working in 1982 at Nucor's new plant near Plymouth, Utah, the
company was just entering the grinding balls business. Cement makers
and mining companies use steel balls in mills that grind minerals into
powder. I was in that job for four years, and it turned out to be a great
experience. I loved every minute of it and worked a lot of hard hours.

One day at a managers' meeting, I got called out to the general manager's office and was told there was somebody on the phone who wanted
to talk to me. It was Dave Aycock, who at the time was president and
COO of Nucor, and Ken Iverson, Nucor's CEO. They had an opening for
a general manager vice president at Nucor-Yamato, and they wanted me.

Nucor-Yamato was—and still is—an innovative partnership with
a great Japanese company. It made sense because our Japanese partners
realized they could be more profitable on U.S. soil than they could exporting from Japan. So that was one benefit of the Plaza Accord. Also,
the Nucor-Yamato deal was a giant leap into territory previously dominated by the big integrated steel companies. The Yamato partnership
was far more ambitious than what those companies were doing—it rep-
resented structural shapes, the large beams and pilings you typically
see in skyscrapers. At the time, only three other U.S. companies made

I-beams that size: Bethlehem, Inland, and U.S. Steel. Today, of course, Bethlehem is gone and Inland's been acquired.

On balance, the Reagan years were good for Nucor and good for U.S. trade policy. Reagan often said he was a free trader, but he knew how to use a tariff when it counted. For example, to save the great American Harley-Davidson motorcycle company, Reagan persuaded Congress to impose a 45 percent tariff on Japanese motorcycles. He was called a protectionist for doing it, but he was right. He was right to save American jobs, and he was right to save an iconic American company. It was good for Harley-Davidson and good for the country.

CHINA RISES

President Reagan's focus on winning the Cold War and reining in the excesses of trade with Japan and West Germany had an interesting, if unintended, consequence: the United States moved closer to China. China and the Soviet Union were bitter enemies. If "the enemy of my enemy is my friend," then cultivating a friendship with China gave America an advantage in the Cold War.

In the previous decades, as U.S. leaders ignored the ballooning problem of Japanese and West German currency manipulation, American manufacturers began looking for other ways to compete on an unequal playing field. Because union contracts, labor costs, and regulations increased the costs of doing business in the United States, manufacturers began looking for a place to make their products more cheaply so they could compete effectively with German- and Japanese-subsidized industries. And many found it in China.

FIGURE 3.3   LOW LABOR COSTS REALITY

While wages are just 10% of those in the United States . . .

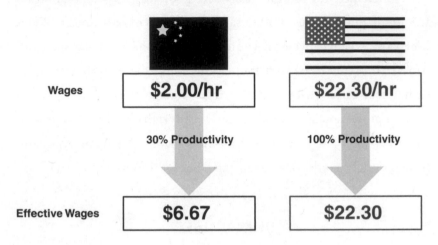

Effective wages are actually **3 times higher** when accounting for productivity

Source: *Boston Consulting Group, "Made In America, Again," August 2011, http:// www.bcg.com/documents/file84471.pdf.*

Reagan's departure from the White House in 1989 signaled a turn in American trade policy as well as in U.S.-China relations. America's relationship with China soured in June of that year, when the Chinese government crushed a peaceful prodemocracy movement in Beijing's Tiananmen Square, killing hundreds and imprisoning thousands more. The massacre exposed Americans to a side of the Chinese government they hadn't seen since the 1960s and put human rights at the forefront of the trade discussion.

Despite the Tiananmen massacre, George H. W. Bush, and later Bill Clinton, took a more open approach to China in an attempt to access the billion-person market for U.S. consumer goods. But something funny happened: China didn't respond in kind. Instead, Beijing promoted mercantilist policies that protected domestic manufacturing. Mercantilism is an old idea in economics. When we think of mercantilism, we usually think of England and Spain in the sixteenth or seventeenth centuries, trying to amass as much gold and silver as they could get their hands on. A mercantilist trading policy is one in which a government protects and heavily subsidizes key industries, exporting as much as possible and importing as little as possible. The great Scottish philosopher and economist Adam Smith said the remedy to mercantilism was laissez-faire capitalism. The "invisible hand" of capitalism has always struggled with the heavy hand of government meddling.

The U.S. trade deficit, which had fallen 60 percent during Reagan's second term and into the elder Bush's presidency, began to expand again in the early 1990s.[7] The move toward free trade (which we'll discuss at greater length in chapter 5) left U.S. industries vulnerable once again to predatory foreign trade practices. With nearly $4 trillion in foreign currency reserves, the Chinese undervalue their own currency—the renminbi—by an estimated 10 percent.[8] That amounts to a sizeable subsidy on its exports and is far more valuable than any savings on labor costs. It's estimated that revaluing China's currency the way Japan and West Germany did in 1985 would create more than 2 million jobs and cut our trade deficit by $71.4 billion over a decade.[9]

We're paying a steep price for the first Bush and Clinton administrations' policies that embraced unrestricted trade. It's no surprise that

FIGURE 3.4   CHINA'S ECONOMIC GROWTH

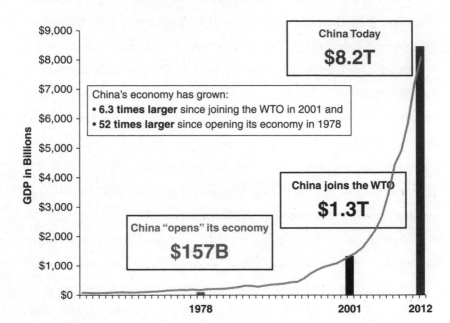

Source: *World Bank, "World Development Indicators," http://data.worldbank.org/ indicator/NY.GDP.MKTP.KD.*

Presidents Bush and Clinton championed the North American Free Trade Agreement, which opened the way for U.S. companies to relocate to Mexico, where labor costs were considerably lower. Clinton was the head cheerleader for creating the World Trade Organization in the early 1990s. And when it came to trade with China, nobody was more insistent about "permanent normal trade relations," with no checks and balances, than Clinton.[10]

China went to the United States and the new WTO and said, "Let us in! We're enlightened! We want to be part of this great system you've built!" But it's worth recalling how Clinton sold the United States on admitting China to the WTO. "We do nothing," Clinton said. "They have to lower tariffs. They open up telecommunications for investment. They allow us to sell cars made in America in China at much lower tariffs. They allow us to put our own distributorships there. They allow us to put our own parts there. We don't have to transfer technology or do joint manufacturing in China any more. This is a hundred-to-nothing deal for America when it comes to the economic consequences."[11]

Not exactly. It's true that today U.S. automakers sell a lot of cars they make in China to Chinese consumers, which as of 2012 is the largest automobile market on the planet. That's a good thing. But Clinton's other predictions never quite panned out, did they? I think it's fair to say the Chinese seduced Clinton—and many other Americans. The good news is, as we'll see, a lot of people know better now.

But 15 years ago, a lot of well-intentioned people assumed that if the Chinese wanted to be part of the WTO badly enough, they'd have to improve their human rights record, start treating their citizens better than serfs, and eventually embrace democratic reforms. Also, if China wanted into the rapidly globalizing world economy, the Chinese would have to stop ripping off American products and pirating our software, movies, and music.

But China figured out pretty quickly that anything Japan and Germany did to take advantage of the open U.S. economy, they could do better. In fact, the Chinese have been far more effective, because they never tried to hide the fact that all of their businesses are government-owned.

What's amazing is how we've let China get away with imposing its mercantilist practices on the rest of the world. We've lost sight of what's necessary to preserve and expand a vibrant, long-lasting economy. Of course, everything the Chinese have done makes perfect sense—for the Chinese. China's leaders have simply and exclusively looked out for their own long-term interests—a natural instinct. Shouldn't we take a page from their playbook and do likewise?

U.S. manufacturers went abroad to communist China because they saw no other way to do business effectively at home in the land of the free. The Chinese government, which in 1978 began its decades-long effort to "liberalize" and co-opt free-market principles for collectivist ends, was more than happy to have American companies bring First World technology to their Third World nation.

Consider what China brought to the table. Here is a big country, with a surplus of cheap labor and hardly any of the regulations that raise costs on companies in the United States and Europe. Chinese authorities have few qualms about moving a million people out of a valley to build a dam and start generating hydroelectric power for new factories and mills. They can bring massive human resources to bear, with wages far below what a company would need to pay in the United States.

What does that mean in practice? Well, if I'm a desperate manufacturer looking for a way to survive, I don't have to worry about unions, burdensome regulations, or excessive taxation. I've got people who seem to actually want me in their country, who are going to welcome me with open arms.

China also held out the promise of opening its market to foreign products. The lure of more than a billion potential new customers is awfully seductive, right? Given the way the U.S. government was allowing our trading partners to have huge cost advantages while undermining profitability of home-based companies, it's hardly surprising many of those companies moved their operations overseas, even to a communist country. For many firms, it was a simple matter of survival.

Ten years ago, I started telling anyone who would listen that there would come a day of reckoning in China. But I also made the perfectly straightforward point that the Chinese have not behaved honorably, and communist governments are not our friends. Behind the welcoming façade of tax breaks and incentives, we've seen widespread cases of corruption, bribery, and blackmail.

I told my colleagues at the Business Roundtable who have operations there that the moment China gets what it needs—technology, best practices, proprietary knowledge, you name it—the Chinese will make their lives miserable over there, just as they're making our lives miserable over here.

Well, guess what? They're starting to see it now. Not everyone. The U.S. business community is far from united on this point, and it's easy to understand why some companies would be reluctant to turn their backs on their investments in China. But the tide may be starting to turn.

Talk to business leaders who have moved their operations to China, particularly the second- and third-tier suppliers who were coaxed into relocating by manufacturers who were already there. Many of them are doing everything they can to get out of China today. Revlon, the cosmetics maker, announced at the end of 2013 it would leave China.

Seesmart, a California-based LED manufacturer, is expanding its operations in Illinois rather than China, where it had outsourced for years. Even Caterpillar, which has a large presence in China, started making machinery in the United States again, citing growing demand here.

But it isn't just about demand. I noticed a change in just the last couple of years. I would see a company president at a roundtable meeting, and he would come up and say, "You were right all along about China. They can't be trusted." After a while, I stopped keeping track of all the stories about Corporation Z or Company X that was lured to China, only to find after a few years that the Chinese government would offer better incentives and more lucrative breaks to a new, Chinese-owned company making the same products, in nearly identical factories, often just across the road.

At one meeting, a government-affairs man and assistant to the CEO of a major U.S. exporter came up to me and said, "You ought to be feeling pretty good about yourself. You're the only guy from the only company raising these issues about China, and you were right. And we were wrong."

"Wait a minute," I replied. "Are you saying this, or is this your boss saying this?" He said his boss wouldn't come out publicly, but the company has figured out China's agenda and has started to respond accordingly. Now, I'm not one to say "I told you so." But I'm glad people are starting to listen. Frankly, we could use better listeners in Washington.

It would be easy to say these companies are acting out of cowardice and greed, but that wouldn't be fair. These are good companies run by well-intentioned people. If you have invested tens or hundreds of millions of dollars overseas, you'd be a fool to anger your hosts. But you might have noticed a number of stories recently about rising labor costs in China. The *Economist* noted back in 2012 that labor costs had increased 20 percent a year over the previous four years. The magazine cited a report by AlixPartners, a consulting firm, which predicted that if China's currency and shipping costs were to rise by 5 percent a year and wages were to go up 30 percent a year, by this year—2015—it would be about as cost effective to manufacture goods in the United States as it would to make the same things in China and ship them over. That prediction wasn't far off. It's becoming more and more expensive to ship freight from China to the United States. A business model of extended supply chains doesn't work when you have a collapsing economy. It just makes things a thousand times worse. The reality is, the Chinese government is making it impossible for these corporations to do business profitably in China. So these companies are having second thoughts, and coming home.

And it's a good thing, too. But don't ever blame a company for trying to make money. Corporations didn't move to China to destroy American jobs. A corporation exists first and foremost to make a profit for its shareholders. If one country passes laws, raises taxes, and erects a wall of work rules and business regulations while another country cuts taxes, carves out exceptions to certain laws, and keeps regulations to a minimum, where would you want to do business? Where are you more likely to fulfill your obligation to your shareholders?

The other question many of these companies tried to resolve was this: How do you compete with countries that we allowed to rig the game, first out of the goodness of our hearts and out of a long-term desire for world peace? In pursuit of that goal, we let the economic system become so distorted that it forced our best and brightest to look elsewhere to set up manufacturing, which is at the core of any healthy economy. All so they could come back, sell goods in their home markets, and compete with Japan, Germany, and other countries that couldn't care less about free trade. We cannot let idealism or ideology blind us to reality.

Hundreds of American companies made investments abroad because failed, shortsighted, and misguided government policies at home made the decision easy for them. There is nothing necessarily wrong with acting in your own interests. Without a doubt, those corporations made decisions that undermined the U.S. economy, undercut real wealth creation, and endangered America's long-term survival as a great power. But they didn't do it out of malice. They did it because well-intentioned American policy makers gave them every reason to. That's the bottom line.

COMPETITIVE ADVANTAGES

In seeking remedies that will restore American manufacturing and construction, it's important for U.S. leaders to recognize a fundamental truth: in order to be globally competitive, you need a stance that combines the best of the private and public sectors. We discussed public-private partnerships in chapter 2. Political leaders also need to adjust their thinking about how states—and nations—compete with each other.

In the United States, all 50 states have been competing against each other for decades. Within states, cities and counties will bend over backward to attract businesses that will create jobs and gin up tax revenues. Weirdly, our federal government hasn't quite figured out that the United States exists in a global state system. Whether it's a state or a nation, they're all working to get the better advantage over their competitors.

If we agree that the basic problem is that the United States losing its ability to innovate things, to make things, and to build things, here is one dimension that makes resolving the problem such a challenge. American companies with large interests overseas will often fight solutions that would make it easier for manufacturing to return to the United States. When I testify before Congress or meet with the president or Senate leaders and say, "Hey, we need to hold China accountable," I'm sure to hear a chorus of other CEOs say, "Oh, God, please don't! The Chinese will kill us!" Not literally. But they're scared out of their wits at what China might do to retaliate, and they demand protections—not for their corporate assets at home, but for investments abroad.

I hate to be the bearer of bad news, but the Chinese are already killing us. It's a death by a thousand cuts. It's the kind of slow death that comes when you allow a country to play by different trading rules than the ones it agreed to in the first place.

Every U.S. corporation understands that rules-based free trade is the way to go, but they've already made big investments over there. If they knew that they weren't going to face retaliation, they wouldn't care. Why? By virtue of their own explanation. Many companies say they're in China to sell diapers and washing machines and copiers to Chinese consumers. That's terrific. We should applaud them. But I don't think it's fair that they make their diapers, or washing machines, or copiers in China, ship them here, and kill more American jobs because the Chinese government gave them special treatment and the United States didn't.

If the federal government doesn't play the game the way our states do, jockeying for more attractive tax laws and policies that make running a business a lucrative enterprise, then we're going to lose. Arkansas is going to lose to Tennessee every day of the week if Arkansas has higher taxes or exorbitant fees. Michigan in December 2012 passed a right-to-work law ending compulsory union membership in part because neighboring Indiana passed an identical law earlier in the year. And businesses by the dozen are leaving California for Texas because of lower taxes and better infrastructure. That's just how the game is played. That's how it should be played! It's the way governments foster a healthy and innovative economy, creating and building things, making real wealth.

REAL WEALTH AND ITS OPPOSITE

In 1889, the great industrialist and steel man Andrew Carnegie published *The Gospel of Wealth,* which argued that men of means had a moral obligation to put their wealth to good use and not to accumulate riches for their own sakes. Carnegie, who was the second-richest man in history after John D. Rockefeller, was also arguably America's greatest philanthropist. Carnegie made his fortune building things and making things. His steel undergirded vast swaths of America's infrastructure—canals, railroads, bridges. Carnegie used his wealth to build America's culture, endowing libraries, universities, and concert halls.

Real wealth is *lasting wealth*. Real wealth creation is a process that reinforces itself. It does not stray from its core to extremes. Real wealth does *not* blow up every four or five years. It reinforces itself, reinvents itself, moves forward, not sideways, and does not create disparities. Carnegie is long dead, but the real wealth he created pays real dividends to this day.

Unfortunately, we've rejected Carnegie's *The Gospel of Wealth* and embraced a far more dangerous, false gospel of wealth that says you

FIGURE 3.5   GROWTH OF FINANCIAL SECTOR

Since 1970 the United States has moved away from creating "real wealth" in manufacturing and construction and toward finance and other services

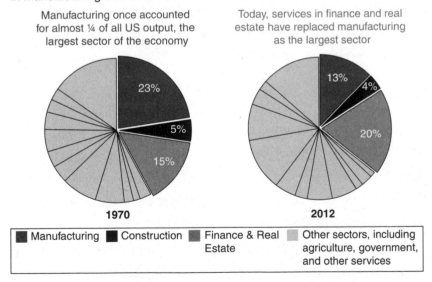

Source: *Bureau of Economic Analysis, "Value Added by Industry as a Percentage of Gross Domestic Product," November 13, 2012, http://www.bea.gov/industry /gdpbyind_data.htm.*

can have something for nothing. For two or three decades or more, the U.S. economy has discouraged manufacturing and encouraged services. And when you review recent economic history, what do you find? Booms and busts, in rapid succession. We've always had economic ups and downs, of course. But when you look at the expansions and recessions since 1970, you find deep and lasting damage to the economy. You find a pattern of well-paying jobs disappearing, to never return, and millions of manufacturing jobs being replaced with service industry jobs or financial industry jobs. You find greed, you find cheating and fraud and a wholesale abandonment of ethics. You find Bernie Madoff and Ken Lay and Dennis Kozlowski. You find bubbles that burst with disastrous consequences. The housing bubble, like every other debt-driven bubble before it, was a giant Ponzi scheme. In reality, for every year that housing prices ballooned, and people found more elaborate ways of packaging financial service "products" that nobody really understood, we lost more ground.

You can manage wealth, certainly. It's important to manage wealth wisely. But you cannot establish a business of selling mortgages to people with low incomes and poor credit, repackage the debt into "mortgage-backed securities," sell it around the world, and expect to last very long. Some people became fantastically "wealthy" on paper. But when the bubble burst in 2008, and over a trillion dollars in housing value simply evaporated, that paper became worthless.

I honestly thought after Lehman Brothers and Washington Mutual and IndyMac and more than 300 other banks went belly-up that we would have finally learned that the road to real wealth isn't paved with speculation and derivatives.

Then again, the lesson didn't sink in after the dot-com bubble burst, or after Enron imploded, or after the savings-and-loan crisis hit. But we need to learn sometime. We need to go back to the basics of sound economic principles. We need to return to the fundamentals of being a nation that innovates, makes, and builds things.

One could argue there are two kinds of capitalism. There is the capitalism that makes and manufactures, and the capitalism that trades and sells. Both have their virtues and can coexist very well together. But a more malicious trading-room capitalism has evolved on Wall Street over the past 20 years. A trader doesn't care whether the company he's buying or selling makes anything. He doesn't care whether it's going in any direction in the long term. He only cares if he makes money today ahead of the other guy tomorrow, or this minute ahead of the next minute. And those are the guys who make the money and reap all of the rewards.

I guess I can't really blame the guys who've been doing the day trading, or who stake hundreds of thousands of leveraged dollars on a trade that occurs in a blink of an eye. They're just responding to an environment that the leadership—whether it's the academic leadership, the business leadership, or the political leadership—has encouraged. Incentives work, even if for the wrong reasons. Just imagine what our economy could look like if we had incentives to encourage investment in real wealth! Imagine if we discouraged poor leadership practices, such as paying corporate executives enormous salaries be it in good times or bad. As I mentioned earlier, that isn't the Nucor way. Everyone shares the pain and everyone shares the gain. If Nucor's stock fell, or we had an off year (as we did in 2009), I took the hit along with everyone else. Pay for performance gives everyone a stake in the company's long-term welfare. How many executives earned six- or seven-figure bonuses in 2008 and 2009, while their companies were going into the toilet and they were closing stores and laying off employees? Those leaders have no real incentive to think beyond the next quarter or the next year. They're going be paid no matter what.

Replacing real wealth creation with short-term thinking—and short-term distortions—is no way to run a business or expand an economy. No matter how much our leaders may try to rationalize it, we know in our guts that these approaches are inherently, morally wrong. Greed and the desire to make more money for the sake of making money, rather than for the sake of building a strong economy—all of that comes from a lack of leadership. And so we end up going down the wrong path.

How do we get back to the right one?

First, you need to throw off the tyranny of short-term thinking and take the long view, just as Carnegie did a century ago, and as Ken Iverson did when he built the team that put Nucor on the path to success. Know your history.

Second, you need the freedom to fail. Engineers learn from failure. Leaders learn from failure. When you see failure, you can't turn a blind eye. You examine it until you understand what went wrong, and then you correct and refine. You need to constantly refine the model—whatever the model is, whether it's business or political or economic—until it works. Then you keep refining it until it works well and keeps you from going down the road to failure again.

It's OK to make mistakes. It's not OK if you don't learn from them. That was a basic tenet of Ken Iverson's philosophy and remains at the heart of Nucor's culture. I tell my team what Ken always said, that I expect they're going to make mistakes. I only have two conditions: First, learn from your mistakes. Second, please make sure it isn't a *really big* mistake. Everyone laughs at that one. Of course, Nucor has made big mistakes before. But we've survived them, precisely because we never made them again.

The United States has made some mistakes, too, going back to the end of World War II. In spite of our best intentions, if not our best efforts, we've seen our economic might ebb and watched in disbelief as a huge gap has developed between the haves and have-nots. Despite years of promises and assurances from our leaders, we've seen the American middle class decline. All of those things happened because smart people, well-intentioned people thought their policies and ideas would have just the opposite outcome. That's what happens when you adhere fanatically to myths and follow a false gospel of wealth.

We need a heavy dose of reality in our education system and in our culture—on the way things really work, so that we can understand, take advantage of, and have the global policy reality work in our favor as opposed to undermining our ability to succeed.

I'm not bashful about saying companies like Nucor are what America needs to be looking at as models of success rather than Wall Street guys. Ultimately, our goal is to re-create a globally competitive economic system in the United States that creates wealth and a revenue stream that encourages investment and reinvestment. That's part of the Nucor culture. The priority is to make money so we can reinvest in our operations, stay competitive, and make more money so we can reward our shareholders and our employees. We pay the right people well and give them a good standard of living because they work hard and efficiently and better than anybody else. That's how it should be: people getting a lot for doing a lot, not getting a lot for doing nothing.

Whether it's Nucor or whether it's a state government or whether it's some other industry, you can never go wrong adhering to these core principles.

FOUR

AGAINST IRRATIONAL DEFEATISM

WHEN I TALK ABOUT THE LOUSY STATE OF THE U.S. economy, I don't mean to sound fatalistic. Do not confuse a clear-eyed assessment of a problem with mere complaining, or doomsaying. Given my training as an engineer, and with four decades in the steel business, my instinct is to look for solutions.

Unfortunately, solutions aren't even part of the debate right now. Many Americans—including people who might be considered experts—have simply thrown up their hands. What do we do? How do we fix this?

I would caution against embracing irrational defeatism—the notion that whatever crises the country might face are beyond solving at this point, and so the best any leader can do is give lip service to the nation's problems. The mood is the opposite of the "irrational exuberance" that former Federal Reserve chairman Alan Greenspan warned of in the mid-1990s, when the tech bubble was inflating. I also don't think government should fix everything. The private sector needs to carry its weight, too.

You've got to live in the market, respond to the market, grow with the market, and use competition to constantly reinvent yourself. Other businesses—and countries—may try to dominate the market, suppress the market, control the market, and distance themselves from competition. I've seen it firsthand, as Nucor steadily expanded throughout the 1980s and 1990s and older, more established steel companies folded and died. They died because they lost touch with what the market wanted. So when the U.S. steel industry goes in one direction, Nucor generally goes in the other, and the rest is history.

When I discuss the economic crisis in front of audiences or on television, I often refer to myself as a "realist" and an "optimist." Realists see things as they are and believe in the possible. Pessimists fixate on the impossible. A pessimist says, "It can't be done. And even if it could be done, it won't work. And even if it works, it won't work *very well*." A realist says, "This is where things are now. Let's figure out a solution." An optimist says, "We can do better, and we will!"

What's the difference between a realist and an optimist? Optimists always look on the bright side. An optimist will say anything is possible. A realist is hopeful, but ultimately practical.

Remember: no problem is unsolvable. *Almost* anything is possible. Some things may be impossible right now, but not tomorrow. So I'm definitely not a pessimist. I'm a realist. And I'm hopeful about the future. But I think we need a heavy dose of realism if we're going to solve the problems in front of us today, right now. You have to be a long-term optimist and, simultaneously, a short- and medium-term realist in order to build real wealth and a successful company or country.

Today's crisis is a massive jobs deficit and an economy ill-equipped to generate the jobs the country needs. Long term, we have a debt crisis, too. But let's focus on today, and prioritize appropriately. No jobs means no economic growth; no economic growth means no tax revenue for government services. The immediate solution is to galvanize the economy and create 30 million jobs.

Pessimists in the press and among the political class are either focused on the wrong problems or offer remedies that are simply too small. Congress spent the weeks after Election Day in 2012 leading up to Christmas trying to negotiate a deal to avert a "fiscal cliff" that they created. By insisting on trying to fix the $16 trillion debt and the multi-trillion dollar budget deficit all at once, politicians from both parties have declined using prudent public investment to address the jobs crisis and the economic crisis. That's exactly the wrong way to solve the problem.

We need to invest wisely and efficiently, in ways that pay back more than what we spend over time. That is, after all, the definition of a successful investment.

Worse than pessimists who serve up small remedies are the defeatists resigned to sluggish and stagnant growth as inevitable. Some economic journalists have taken to calling our current circumstances "the new normal." Lately, the phrase has appeared with some frequency in the *New York Times,* the *Financial Times,* and *Forbes,* and it's commonplace among commentators on CNBC, CBS, and *ABC News*. What's more, analysts from corporations like the fast-food chain McDonald's and major consulting firms like McKinsey say, with certainty, that a low-growth economy is here to stay.

I understand the temptation to give in to such pessimism. Obviously, we haven't created enough jobs in six years, economic growth is well below where it needs to be, and we're missing the visionary leadership we need to turn the crisis around.

In all my years in the steel business, I've gotten pretty good at finding and fixing structural flaws. Once, shortly after I started at Nucor's facility in Plymouth, Utah, we had 37 tons of a 60-ton batch of steel bars fail a crucial mechanical test. Nobody could figure out why some of the bars failed while others didn't, because they all came from the same molten metal. So here this steel was sitting in a warehouse, and we were getting ready to scrap it because it was flawed. This was a multi-million dollar problem. But we couldn't keep making steel bars the same way and hope the steel would somehow pass. We had to find the flaw and fix it.

I had just arrived at Nucor, and I was still pretty new in the industry. Everyone was looking to me like I should have the answer right off the top of my head, but to be honest, I didn't know what the hell was going on. I had a roll mill manager—a guy with 50 years of dirt-under-the-fingernails experience—tell me, "Don't worry about it. Let it sit. It will age, and in a couple of weeks we'll retest it and everything will be fine."

I couldn't do that. Even if the manager happened to be right and the bars retested fine, we still wouldn't know what caused the original failure, and we would keep making the same mistake. Instead, I looked at the chemistry and ran a bunch of regression analyses. It showed what the chemistry looked like on the bars that failed and on bars that passed. The next thing we did was to tighten the melting standards, which, of course, got everyone mad. Two weeks went by. We retested the bars. They all passed. The experienced manager was right, but we still needed a solution for the original failures.

The problem was a fairly technical one involving dissolved gases and diffusion of these gases to safe locations over time. But the shop manager didn't realize the cause. Nobody did. He was content to let the steel settle for a couple of weeks, expecting it would be fine. Never mind how much all that additional wait time would cost the company. We adjusted the process so the metal passed right away; we didn't have to wait weeks, and production could speed up. It was a home run.

So, as it turned out, something that seemed like "the new normal" in fact wasn't.

When I survey the broader economy, the weakness in the manufacturing and construction sectors is easy to see. But those are also areas where opportunities for growth and renewal are greatest.

Millions of unemployed Americans have skills that are going *unused*. They haven't completely forgotten those skills, but they are getting rusty. We need to create jobs again for the skills people have and quit bemoaning the skills they allegedly don't. The problem isn't that we don't have enough of the right people. They're out there. If we need to spend money moving them to where the jobs are in the country, then let's do it. If we need to build factories where the workers are, then let's do it. But create jobs for the skills people have. We have had, and will always have, some misfit in skills as new technologies evolve, but that shouldn't matter.

We hear a lot about solving the problem simply by investing in more research and development. There is an argument, from groups like the Task Force on American Innovation, for the United States to double, triple, or even quadruple its annual spending on R&D, and even make permanent federal tax credits for research. R&D programs are important, and more investment would be a fine idea to foster innovation. But research and development won't get you out of a crisis. R&D takes years—even decades—to yield any benefits. If you want a long-term strategy, yes, by all means, invest in research and development. But you still need to deal with the short-term crisis on its own terms.

I also worry that many political leaders talk about the economy in ways that only distract and divide the American people. The 2012 presidential election was ugly all around, with both Republicans and Democrats demonizing each other. But I was really bothered by the way some candidates demonized business. Ultimately, a strong economy requires business.

One example sticks out in my mind. I had to shake my head when I listened to Elizabeth Warren's speech to the Democratic National Convention in Charlotte. Warren talked about how the American middle class has been "chipped, squeezed and hammered." No argument from me there. But her comments demonized business. "We don't run this country for corporations, we run it for people," she said.[1] I think she misses the more important, if obvious, truth that corporations are what actually put people to work.

Who starts a business? Who forms a corporation? Who hires workers? Who sells products people want and need? People do. A lot of the rhetoric during the election reminded me of the old *Dudley Do-Right* cartoons, where the hero would always rescue his best girl Nell from Snidely Whiplash's latest fiendish plot. It's a cartoon caricature of a villain, nothing more.

The problem with too many political leaders today is they only know how to demonize. When it comes time to face a crisis head on, they don't know how to act. When it comes to solving problems, they do what the pessimists do and fixate on the impossible.

I'm enthusiastic about the natural gas boom underway in the United States. It's no exaggeration to call natural gas a game changer for the U.S. economy, for American business, and for Americans' quality of life. Energy is a huge part of our trade deficit, so developing a massive domestic source would pay huge dividends. Want to get energy independent? Want to stop importing oil from tyrants? Well, we're sitting on top of one of the largest known natural gas reserves on the planet.

And what's happening? Environmentalists who flirted with the idea of natural gas as an alternative to coal have turned against it. They're using all sorts of scare tactics. A recent documentary called *Gasland* shows fire coming out of people's kitchen faucets in towns near gas wells, and argues that fracking pollutes groundwater and allegedly causes other harms. Meantime, government regulators are devising ways to make natural gas more difficult to extract. And now opportunistic politicians are lining up against hydraulic fracturing—aka fracking—which has been around for decades and is perfectly safe.

If you want to revive U.S. manufacturing and slash the trade deficit, at a time when people are becoming disenchanted with doing business in China, and at a time when Europe is wrestling with a major economic meltdown, then you really can't go wrong with stepping up natural gas production and using it to reinvigorate our manufacturing sector.

With the right leadership, we could spur some significant economic growth in the United States, which would spill over to the rest of the world. We could lead the world again. And instead we're fighting over fracking and fiscal cliffs. Even months after the last election, some people were still arguing whether the president of the United States was born in Hawaii, or whether Mitt Romney was a good CEO. Encouraging more rancor isn't helpful. It's not bringing anybody together. But rhetoric designed to divide people instead of bring them together has a direct impact on what's happening with the economy. It has a direct impact on how people in government see themselves as the only answer.

I don't think the government should treat Americans as if they're helpless. Wouldn't we be better off if the public and private sectors thought of themselves as playing on the same team, working toward the same goal?

REALISM VERSUS MYTHOLOGY

All of this is interrelated—the pessimism, the "new normal" negativism, the divisive political rhetoric. It's weighing down the economy. If the prevailing mood in the United States is one of low growth or no growth, with businesses hunkering down rather than investing and growing, then low-growth or no-growth policies will naturally follow. It's that irrational defeatism I talked about earlier.

So as we start discussing a realist's solutions to the crisis, Americans need to reject a few cherished myths and long-held assumptions. We cannot do more of the same and expect different results. One myth is that the international trading system works. Another myth is that America's manufacturing edge is gone forever.

We need to de-emphasize extremes and return to the fundamentals of being a nation that innovates, makes, and builds things. Anyone who says that the United States can create or innovate without being able to make and build isn't a realist. When you get away from manufacturing, and get into the service and service-to-service sector and the financial sector and rely on that to create wealth, you will fail. It will only create one busted bubble after another.

Realists know we need to strengthen and revitalize our manufacturing sector by reducing the trade deficit in goods; we need to produce more of our own energy here at home and buy a lot less of it from overseas.

Where are the opportunities to create the jobs we need in manufacturing and construction? Well, let's look at our deficiencies. Could that big, red, flashing light of a trade deficit offer a clue? The U.S. trade deficit in 2013 totaled $475 billion, meaning we imported that much more in goods and services than we exported.[2] Why do we have a huge trade deficit? Because we've allowed people to distort the trading system. Breaking it down, what does the trade deficit look like? Well, we can say that roughly half of it is in energy and half of it is in goods made elsewhere and sold here.

Realists know there is a crying need for new and refurbished infrastructure in the United States. You can't have a strong economy with crumbling roads and bridges and over-trafficked waterways. Government has a spending problem in a lot of areas, but infrastructure isn't one of them. Rebuilding infrastructure can create millions of jobs and spur revenue growth. But to get there, yes, we're going to need to spend tax dollars, and yes, we're going to need to borrow money. The payback will far exceed the expenditure, and it will last for 50 years or more.

Infrastructure requires steel and concrete and timber. It requires heavy equipment. And it requires manpower. Same story with energy. Developing America's natural gas potential requires lots of people and lots of equipment. If the United States wants to balance its trade deficit, and we should, what better way than to develop our natural gas, using that plentiful and cheap energy source to power manufacturing and put more Americans back to work?

Another myth is the so-called skills gap. The truth is, most skills can be learned on the job. As I'll discuss later, the United States can do better at vocational training, and we need to be doing a lot more with online learning. But I categorically reject any idea that the United States has some sort of unbridgeable skills deficit.

Giving money away won't solve our problems. It's got to be invested in projects that are going to deliver a return over time, that create revenues, and that help us deal with our spending excesses and our budget shortfalls. So government can either be part of the problem or part of the solution. Right now, government is part of the problem—a huge part. You've probably heard a lot about how government regulates too much or too little. Both claims are true. Government overregulates some industries and underregulates others. Mainly, government regulates badly.

What's worse, we spend tax money foolishly. Republicans and Democrats fought like cats and dogs over the 2009 stimulus. The truth is, the stimulus was a failure, but not for the reasons most people think. The stimulus could have worked if most of that spending had remained in the United States. It didn't.

More on that in chapter 7. But first, let's delve deeper into the myths and realities of free trade.

FIVE

THE MYTH OF
FREE TRADE

THE U.S. ECONOMY WAS IN CRITICAL CONDITION in February 2009. Before the month was over, another 724,000 Americans would be unemployed.[1] The month before, 818,000 Americans lost their jobs.[2] Those losses came on top of the 2.6 million Americans out of work by the end of 2008.[3] President Obama had only been on the job for a couple of weeks, but he was already neck-deep in a fight with Congress.

At issue was the president's $787 billion economic stimulus package. Democrats and Republicans battled fiercely over the contents of the plan. Should there be more tax cuts? More spending? How about subsidies for green jobs? Or maybe more money for public education?

Should the federal government bail out cash-strapped state governments to halt layoffs of public-sector workers? What about more infrastructure spending?

At $105 billion, infrastructure turned out to be a large part of the package—but not nearly large enough. As the stimulus debate dragged on, a new term entered the national lexicon: "shovel-ready jobs." For the stimulus to actually *stimulate* the U.S. economy, those billions of dollars would need to go to projects that have already cleared the years-long permitting and approval process. For the stimulus to reverse the rising unemployment rate, government would need to get those dollars into the economy quickly. I found myself in the national spotlight as Congress debated what the stimulus package should look like. Remember, the most important thing the federal government needed to do in 2009 was restart the U.S. economy. That's what the stimulus fight was about. But the money needed to stay in the United States. Because of the distortions in our economy, the federal government's attempt to resolve the jobs crisis had major implications around the globe. Foreign trade was a poorly understood part of the stimulus debate. The U.S. business community split on how Congress could best help the economy. So I sat down with Leslie Stahl of *60 Minutes* to explain why Congress should include a "Buy American" clause in the stimulus package.

My argument was pretty simple. If you want to create jobs and get the economy going again, you need to make sure we're investing in American companies and American workers. All I asked was that Congress make certain that states taking stimulus-related tax dollars for roads and bridge repair and power grid upgrades spend the money in the United States, where it was needed most. What would be the point of spending hundreds of billions of tax dollars only to stimulate the economies of China, Germany, Mexico, and all of those other countries?

But the "Buy American" clause received a lot of pushback from CEOs who do business abroad, Caterpillar and General Electric in particular. Eventually, President Obama came out against the language, saying, "We can't send a protectionist message" to the rest of the world. Most Republicans opposed it, too.

In the middle of our interview, Stahl asked, "What happens if all these countries that sell steel to us—China, Russia, Brazil—say OK, well, we're just not going to buy Caterpillar products, we're not going to take in John Deere products, we're not going to take in GE products." In other words, what if "Buy American" set off a crippling trade war?

And I said, "Fear of a trade war is one of those scary trump phrases that free traders use to shut up their critics: 'Please don't talk about defending American businesses against unfair and illegal trade practices, or we'll end up in a trade war!'"[4] I told Stahl that we're in a trade war already. But the trade war is being waged on us. When you don't hold nations accountable for not playing by the rules they agreed to when they joined the World Trade Organization and Congress granted them most favored nation trading status, opening our markets to their goods while our companies struggle under quotas and ownership restrictions, you're basically saying, "Anything goes."

I said it on *60 Minutes* in 2009, and I'm telling you again now: we're in a trade war, and we're letting our competitors win. The American people shouldn't stand for it.

WHY FREE TRADE DOESN'T WORK

Fear of trade wars goes hand in hand with an unquestioning faith in the ideology of free trade. For more than 60 years, the United States has pursued trade policies that have exaggerated our deficits with Japan, Germany, China, and the rest of the world, undercut our manufacturing base, exploded our national debt, depressed wages, and made the American middle class poorer even as our gross domestic product has grown. But that wasn't what advocates of free trade promised.

In theory, free trade is a system where goods, money, and labor move freely among nations without barriers. Genuine free trade allows for no tariffs or taxes, no subsidies or quotas. The idea is free trade lowers costs and boosts innovation by promoting unfettered competition. And free trade is supposed to make everyone richer, more equal, and improve global security because countries that are selling to each other aren't likely shooting at one another.

Free trade turns on the theory of comparative advantage, which says a country has an advantage in producing a commodity—it could be clothing, could be steel—if the opportunity costs of production are lower. Under the theory laid out nearly 200 years ago by British economist David Ricardo, countries could be pretty good at producing something (he used the examples of English textiles and Portuguese wine), but the country that is marginally better has the comparative advantage and should specialize in that thing. The idea is that everyone will gain and nobody will lose, because free trade ensures that the only transactions are mutually beneficial ones.

I reject this conventional wisdom about free trade. Free trade is a beautiful idea. Too bad it doesn't exist outside the cozy confines of academia and the mainstream media. In the real world, we don't have free trade. We've never had free trade. At best, we have managed trade. At worst, we have predatory and protectionist countries unfairly exploiting our belief in free trade to their advantage.

When governments get involved and stack the deck in their own favor instead of letting comparative advantage rule, then you have distorted trade. Call it free trade all you like, but it isn't so.

My career has spanned a period when U.S. leaders have outright ignored sound trade policy in the name of free trade. When I started out as a young engineer in the 1970s, we were in conflict with Japan and Germany over steel and cars. In those days, if you worked for a U.S. steel company, unionized or not, you didn't buy a foreign car. And if you did drive a foreign car onto a plant site, whether it was a mill or a research lab or whatever, you took a lot of crap. The only thing worse than working for an American steel company and driving a foreign car would have been working for Ford and driving a Chevy.

Looking back over 40 years, it's clear that the arguments for free trade, which sounded so nice in economics class, haven't panned out in the real world. Sure, eliminating barriers to U.S. goods has an obvious appeal. Who wouldn't want to get rich selling their products to people all over the world? And you can understand why we gave the Europeans and Japanese a break, because those places had to be rebuilt after World War II. We were the only major industrial power that hadn't been destroyed. But we shouldn't fool ourselves. What incentive do other countries really have to avoid predatory practices? Where are the penalties? The only penalties are to American economic growth and national interest.

Consider Japan again. The island was a smoking ruin after World War II. The United States had every advantage. Yet even in 1955, when the United States negotiated the first post-occupation trade deal there, the Japanese did not act like a conquered people. American negotiators argued that Japan should cut its tariffs on auto imports because the United States was the world's leading automaker, so it would be to Japan's advantage to simply import U.S. cars and specialize in export goods wherein Japan had a comparative advantage. In response, Japan's chief trade negotiator wrote, "If the theory of international trade were pursued to its ultimate conclusion, the United States would specialize in the production of automobiles and Japan in the production of tuna."[5] Japan said it would produce cars *and* package tuna while protecting and encouraging key domestic industries. In short, free trade was a luxury that Japan decided it could not afford. Negotiations ended with both sides making concessions. However, the United States failed to gain equal reciprocity in the negotiations, and privately some officials conceded that the importance of a thriving Japan to U.S. containment policy was used to our disadvantage.

Japan found it could excel in the international markets by making its exports cheaper than everyone else's. In the United States, costs were high and labor was expensive. Japan didn't have an advantage in human capital or industrial capacity. But the Japanese learned how to keep the value of the yen very low by manipulating its currency so that it was valued four or five times below the dollar. So the United States allowed

Japan to manipulate its currency in order to become cost competitive, develop an export strategy, and create jobs without regard to how such a policy would hurt American industries over the long term. It's no surprise we went from a nation where manufacturing made up 25 percent of its GDP in the mid-1960s to 12.5 percent today.[6]

Again and again, we let the Japanese and the Germans benefit improperly from our willingness to help them get back on their feet. We should have said, "Enough is enough! Value your currency properly and stop taking advantage of us, or we will hold you accountable."

Now, of course, we're no longer dealing with small, democratic nations like Japan and Germany. Instead, we're trying to compete with a massive country of 1.3 billion people and an authoritarian government that demands political stability at all costs. The Chinese government maintains order by creating jobs—and forcing people to work in them. They've done everything possible to increase manufacturing, just as we've done everything possible in this country to diminish it.

U.S. political leaders like to describe the relationship between the United States and China as a "partnership" or a "strategic partnership." Such language might be fine for the sake of international diplomacy, but it obscures the facts. The Chinese are mercantilist and predatory trade competitors. They aren't partners.

Now, please don't misunderstand me. The problem isn't that China is getting rich building its economy. That's fine. That's what every government is supposed to do for its citizens. (If only our leaders would do the same!) No, the problem is we've aided China's growth by laying waste to our manufacturing sector and our middle class. China's growth mustn't come at our expense. Americans are the largest consumer of Chinese-made products on the planet. They need us as much as we need them.

Truth is, we've been in a trade conflict with China since the mid-1990s, when Beijing began pegging its currency to the dollar after devaluing its currency by 87 percent. In addition to effectively subsidizing exports by manipulating the yuan, China's government gives its industries an advantage through direct and indirect subsidies to businesses, export grants, tax breaks for some favored industries, and tax levies on disfavored imports, along with import quotas, technology mandates, and ownership restrictions. According to a study by the Economic Policy Institute, China's currency manipulation alone has cost the United States more than 2.1 million manufacturing jobs and has added $217 billion to our trade deficit.[7]

This is modern-day mercantilism, plain and simple.

Trade mercantilism is all about governments doing things to promote trade to bring money back home so they can build armies. That's really what it's boiled down to over history. Beginning with the creation of the British East India Company, the British sought to protect the interest of its merchants and the Crown's pocketbook, all in the name of preserving its global power. And it's perfectly rational. It makes sense for a developing country like China to do everything it can to protect its industries from competition so they can grow and flourish.

I hate to use the word *protect*, because its meaning has been so distorted and bastardized by free-trade advocates. But if countries have a right to develop their economies, then they should also have a right to make sure trade is conducted according to certain mutually

FIGURE 5.1   IMPACTS OF CHINA'S CURRENCY MANIPULATION

The yuan has appreciated **10%** since June 2010, but many
economists still feel the currency is undervalued

| Every 1% rise in the yuan. . . | . . . cuts China's global surplus by **$17 to $25 billion** . . . | . . . and lowers the US deficit by **$2.5 to $6 billion** over the following two to three years |

| Jobs Lost to China Since 2001
2.7 million | Currency manipulation exacerbates the US trade deficit with China and has caused the loss of more than 2.7 million American jobs since 2001 — including more than 2.1 million manufacturing jobs |

Source: *William R. Cline, "Renminbi Undervaluation, China's Surplus, and the US Trade Deficit," Peterson Institute, http://www.piie.com/publications/pb/pb10-20 .pdf; Robert E. Scott, "The China Toll," Economic Policy Institute, August 23, 2012, http://www.epi.org/publication/bp345-china-growing-trade-deficit-cost/.*

agreed-upon rules. If you want free trade, you can't have mercantilism. If you want mercantilism, you can't have free trade.

No discussion of free trade is complete without a mention of Scottish moral philosopher Adam Smith, whose free-trade theories—laid out in his most famous book, *The Wealth of Nations*—came about in reaction to British mercantilism. "If a foreign country can supply us with a commodity cheaper than we ourselves can make it," Smith wrote, "better buy it from them with some part of the produce of our own industry, employed in a way in which we have some advantage."[8]

When you read Smith, remember that Great Britain could only afford to embrace free trade after centuries of building up its economy under the mercantilist system. They weren't pie-in-the-sky idealists. They were realists.

Countries like China, Japan, Russia, Germany, India, Singapore, and South Korea have balanced their supposed acceptance of global free trade with a healthy dose of common sense. So, unlike the United States, a country like Brazil will put up barriers to importing certain goods, like textiles and steel products, from countries like China that effectively game the world trading system. They use all of the tried-and-true nontariff barriers—quotas, value-added taxes, the works. And they practice protectionism to guard against being overwhelmed by predatory, mercantilistic trading practices. They're realists too.

The best way I can explain China's predatory and mercantilist trade practices would be from my perspective as a steel man. China's production of steel went from 100 million tons a year to over 700 million tons in less than a decade. They flooded the market.

In January 2009, the same month 800,000 Americans lost their jobs, Chinese-made steel plate cost half as much as U.S.-made steel plate. In the darkest months of the recession, as construction ground to a halt and demand plummeted, imports of finished Chinese steel to the United States increased sharply. That didn't happen by accident or by nature. China was selling below cost on the international market. That's called dumping, and it's illegal under the General Agreement on Tariffs and Trade.

In 2009, the International Trade Commission backed a U.S. Commerce Department finding that American steel companies had been harmed by Chinese subsidies for $2.8 billion in imported steel pipe meant for oil and natural gas wells.[9] As a result, the Commerce Department imposed a 13.2 percent duty on those products. That same year, Commerce placed new duties on Chinese aluminum after finding China had subsidized $514 million in exports. Yet the Commerce Department avoids other, more damaging findings—namely, that China's currency manipulation is the greatest subsidy of all.

Without question, China dumps steel in the United States and all around the world. But it faces virtually no consequences. Nucor has filed dumping complaints against China. So have other steel companies and countries. So has the U.S. government. Once in a while, we win. But not nearly often enough to deter them.

China has no comparative advantage to produce steel. Now, it might seem so because of the lower labor costs and lack of regulation. You'll say, well of course it's cheaper to produce steel in China. It's not, and if it is, it's only by a small margin. So how does China sell so much steel to the United States? Easy. By breaking international trade agreements.

Steel is low cost in America because it's not especially labor-intensive. It's energy-intensive and raw material–intensive. Nucor is extremely efficient with energy, and remember, we recycle scrap to make our steel. Start to finish, one ton of steel sheet takes 0.4 man-hours per ton, or a labor cost of $8 to $10 per ton.

China imports raw materials and energy to make its steel. The freight to get the steel from China to the United States is $40 a ton. I don't care what your labor costs are—they could be zero—there is no way you can make up for that $32 differential without cheating. It's flat-out impossible.

China's steel industry is obviously subsidized. They're producing nearly 820 million tons of steel per year, and they're losing money. That's how out of control it is. Yet China continues to overbuild because Beijing wants to maintain the jobs that go into constructing the steel plants, and eventually maintain the smaller number of jobs running these highly automated facilities.

Yet we can't sell steel to China. The barriers to entry are too high. Market forces aren't allowed to work. We can't build a steel mill in China, although China can certainly build steel mills here. If you don't believe me, ask Lakshmi Mittal, the chairman, CEO, and principal owner of ArcelorMittal, the world's biggest steel company. He wanted to buy a controlling stake in Hunan Valin Steel, one of the major Chinese steel manufacturers. He couldn't do it. Beijing will not allow foreign ownership of key industries.

China's economic practices seem strange to us because we believe so strongly in the free market. We believe in fair play. Most of us still believe in a good, old-fashioned profit motive. Yet we see China rising fast, on the brink of replacing the United States as the world's largest economy and profiting in almost every business it touches, even though they're not free and don't play fair.

Let's face it, most of the world doesn't really believe in an open-market philosophy like we do. When China cheats, they deny Americans economic opportunity. We really shouldn't sit still for that.

I don't believe the United States needs to copy or emulate everything—or perhaps anything—China does. But I do think we need to be more insistent in holding others to international standards. We don't talk about international trade *suggestions*. If you believe in free markets, you must believe in rules. Free markets cannot exist without honest-to-goodness, legally binding contracts.

For too long our faith in free trade has been governed less by confidence in our ability to compete than by fear of what our competitors will do to us if we insist on enforcing the rules. How many times have you heard a CEO or a congressman say that if we don't have an open market to China and allow Chinese firms to come in here and invest, they're not going to let us into China to invest?

I've heard a million variations on the argument. I attend these Business Roundtable meetings in Washington, D.C., and it doesn't matter who shows up to speak—it could be an economics professor from Harvard or it could be the president of the United States. The question is always the same: "What are you going to do to protect us from retaliation in China if we force them to play by a set of rules?"

Companies like Boeing, Procter & Gamble, and Xerox all have huge investments overseas, so they have an incentive to oppose U.S. government efforts to seek relief from the World Trade Organization for U.S.-based manufacturers. They're understandably fearful of retaliation. Does it matter that Chinese companies are all state-owned or controlled? Does it matter that the Chinese don't do business the same way Americans do? Of course it does. Beijing isn't going to let American companies invest unless the government benefits. And then China is going to undermine the investments Americans make and kick us out as soon they can.

Think I'm exaggerating? The Chinese government told Boeing and Airbus in 2012 that it would stop buying passenger aircraft from them in the next five years, because the state-owned Commercial Aircraft of China Corporation is going to make all of China's airplanes going forward. Now, where do you think the Chinese learned how to make those planes? At the same time, you might have heard about Boeing and Airbus suffering delays and cost overruns for their next generation of passenger aircraft. All of those problems occurred in their overseas factories.

We've tried quiet diplomacy. It's failed miserably. We've tried to publicly shame China into stopping its illegal currency manipulation. President Obama appealed directly to Chinese leaders. China's leaders flatly denied they're doing anything wrong. And in the face of all evidence, the U.S. Treasury Department and the Commerce Department still refuse to label China as a currency manipulator.

Where is the World Trade Organization in all of this? The WTO in 1995 replaced the General Agreement on Tariffs and Trade with the idea of creating a formal process of resolving global trade disputes. The WTO is a noble experiment in the tradition of the League of Nations, the Kellogg-Briand nonaggression pact of 1928, and the United Nations. The UN passes resolutions but can do little to enforce them. The WTO is similar. It's one thing to get a large group of countries to sign a piece of paper agreeing that the world would be better off practicing free trade under a certain set of rules. But none of those countries that signed on to the WTO abandoned a domestic policy that put their interests above all others.

Think about the United Nations for a minute. If you're one of 167 voices and you can't exercise the influence that the size of your economy would suggest, then you're at a disadvantage. At the end of the day, self-interest prevails. The same goes for the WTO. The only way the WTO works is if more nations realize it's better to cooperate with the United States than it is to cooperate with the Chinese.

That's starting to happen—a backlash is beginning as more countries are beginning to feel the effects of China's extreme form of mercantilism. Suddenly, it isn't just the world's sole superpower that is feeling market pressure from Beijing.

STANDING UP TO CHEATERS

If anything good has come of the current financial crisis, it's been the awakening of a few more business leaders and politicians to America's trade problem. If the question is how we are supposed to create jobs, then trade must be part of the solution.

So even though America's leaders aren't yet focused on the problem the way I'd like, I give Barack Obama and Mitt Romney credit for making China's currency manipulation and the U.S. trade deficit an issue in the 2012 presidential election campaign. The two candidates certainly disagreed on the scope of the problem, and, as the challenger, Romney could speak more bluntly about Chinese abuses than Obama could. But it was heartening to hear both parties talk about manufacturing and trade in a way they never had before.

The good news is both sides of the political aisle agree that America cannot let China keep cheating because we've got to rebuild our manufacturing base. Now, standing up to cheaters can be tough. The tendency of an international body like the WTO is to make a lot of rules and then selectively enforce them. Most countries would naturally rather hold their competitors to a different standard than themselves.

Well, Reagan didn't mind ensuring that everyone played on a level field. It's really not that hard. Reagan recognized that if nations want access to our markets, we should expect reciprocation. But other than a few small protests and limited agreements over the years, it really wasn't until the Reagan years that the United States took the lead in demanding conformity to international trade agreements. It took the leadership of Reagan to show the world that free trade is great only when nations practice it *with accountability.*

When countries break the rules, the United States needs to take a page from the old Reagan playbook. When Reagan negotiated the Plaza Accord and made Japan and Germany revalue their currencies and be subject to market forces, not government manipulation, we had 20 years of strong economic growth as a result.

So the United States needs to tell the WTO that we will take action to stop anything that is not consistent with rules-based free trade. And if the WTO is going to remain viable, it had damn well better prove that it can enforce the letter of the law, as opposed to looking the other way. It's not enough to repeat *free trade* as an empty mantra while countries prey on open markets.

Historically, the United States hasn't been shy about taking care of its interests. We've won world wars, we've put men on the moon, and we've floated a navy that has kept the sea-lanes free and open for nearly a century. We've got to be willing to say, right now, no more cheating. And if the WTO won't act, the U.S. government should. We have the tools. We should use them.

THE NEED FOR GOVERNMENT-TO-GOVERNMENT SOLUTIONS

The U.S. government should not leave it up to private companies to defend themselves against state-owned enterprises. Here's another area where a public-private partnership would do some good.

Our government needs to sit down with the business community and say, "We know what the rules are. We're going to be policing them now. This is how we're going to support the private sector. We're going to police this for you." And in turn, the private sector needs to make sure the government is on the case. But the government needs to take steps to make sure private enterprise isn't irreparably harmed before the United States takes action. Any solution has got to be a government-to-government, not a private-company-to-government, solution.

Believe it or not, many corporations are at a disadvantage—particularly corporations that play by the rules and want to make and sell products in the United States. Right now, it's possible for companies to bring unfair trading practice complaints against foreign companies and governments to the WTO. It's also very tough to do—time consuming and very expensive. By law, a company must prove it has been "damaged" before it can file a complaint. And even then, a complaint takes about two years to resolve. That's two years' worth of additional damages. Companies go out of business before their cases are ever heard.

In the early 2000s, the steel industry was once again under serious threat from illegal Chinese dumping. Thirty-two U.S. companies were in bankruptcy, and the industry was looking to Washington for help—and it wasn't getting much. The prevailing attitude toward the

steel business among a lot of politicians and policy makers was not unlike the mistaken view my engineering buddies and I held in the early
1970s: U.S. steel was a dying industry not worth mourning. In that environment, I was named chief executive officer of Nucor.

We had avoided trade disputes and politics generally. But the industry as a whole was in crisis, and I decided Nucor should get more
heavily involved with the American Iron and Steel Institute, which is
the industry's main trade association. For a long time, the chairman of
the AISI was Tom Usher, who was also chairman, president, and CEO
of U.S. Steel. Usher was smart enough to know that on trade issues, the
Bethlehems and the U.S. Steels had a very bad image in Washington.
Nucor was just the opposite. In 40 years, we had only filed one trade
action—and that was in 1998, when I was manager of Nucor-Yamato
Steel. So we weren't in the habit of asking for government relief.

Usher had the idea that I should take over as chairman of the AISI.
He was pretty adamant about it, actually. He thought I would be a far
more credible voice on behalf of the steel industry, precisely because
Nucor had grown and succeeded even in the face of unfair foreign competition. And so my first major act as chairman of the AISI was to address the World Steel Industry conference in Berlin. And I told them:
That's enough. We aren't going to sit idly by and let the U.S. steel industry disappear. We are going to take action, because our very survival is
at stake.

Soon after the Berlin speech, several representatives from the remaining U.S. steel companies and I sat down with President George W.
Bush to discuss what needed to be done to save this major American
industry. Treasury Secretary Paul O'Neill, Commerce Secretary Don

Evans, and U.S. Trade Representative Robert Zoellick were also present. We made our case. And during a break afterward, Evans walked over to me, grabbed me by the arm, pulled me aside, and said, "Listen, Dan, the only reason we're giving you the time of day as an industry is because you're taking the lead. Otherwise, I'm telling you, we would not be supporting your efforts. But we know that if Nucor is complaining, something is really, really wrong."

And that's where, as a leader, your job is to make sure you use all of the resources you have at your disposal when the time is right. You can't waste your capital on small fights. For years—decades, really—the steel industry ran to Washington for help at the first hint of trouble. But the Washington consensus changed to favor the ideology of free trade, no matter how distorted a version it might be.

Our leadership role and our reputation helped sway an administration biased toward free trade to support the steel industry on a massive trade dispute. And it was a big one. Everybody in the world got shook up by it—customers, farms, steel producers, trading companies, you name it. But it was a necessary fight, and it worked. President Bush in 2002 agreed to place a one-year tariff on foreign steel ranging from 8 percent to 30 percent.

That got us through a very difficult time. And, by the way, all of the predictions of a massive trade war turned out to be completely unfounded. The economy took off again in 2004, and the rest, as they say, is history.

We won an important victory, but I learned a valuable lesson in the process. No individual company can compete against state-owned enterprises and other governments. It takes cooperation between the private sector and the public sector to do that, and we haven't seen enough of that sort of action in the United States. I firmly believe in the adage that you can't fight city hall, whether the city hall is Beijing or Washington or Moscow.

When it comes right down to it, what was the steel industry asking the federal government to do? Enforce the rules—and that's it. I've never asked Congress to give Nucor a handout, and I wasn't asking the government to bail out the steel industry. All I was saying was: Do your job as a government and make sure your private sector isn't taken advantage of by another government.

More U.S. manufacturers should seek a level playing field the way the steel industry did. And if it takes an industrial policy to do it, then that's what Congress should do. But the worst thing is to let someone else have an industrial policy while we talk about free trade. If we believe in free enterprise, if we believe in free trade, and if we believe that the best team wins, we've got to do things that help us to be the best team. Being the best team doesn't mean cheating. All it really means is ensuring the global playing field is as level as it can be.

If you stop and think about it, the steel industry is the canary in the coal mine. And we've worked hard to get other CEOs and business leaders and elected officials to understand that the challenges to the steel industry aren't unique; they can happen to other industries. That's like Republic or U.S. Steel saying, *Oh, that's just Nucor; they're in the rebar business. They won't catch up to us. They won't dominate the steel industry someday. We're safe.*

Don't you believe it.

SIX

THE MYTH OF THE INNOVATION ECONOMY AND THE "SKILLS GAP"

MANY AMERICANS BELIEVE THE COUNTRY'S FUture rests firmly in the realm of innovation. We're a creative society, after all. A comprehensive list of American innovations—from acrylic paint and the artificial heart to the Ziploc bag—could probably fill an entire book.

So why can't the United States simply invent its way out of the current economic crisis? As it happens, a broad consensus of U.S. political and business leaders believes we must be an innovative economy, that we're not innovative enough, and that we need to innovate more, even at the expense of manufacturing.

President Obama is foremost among the cheerleaders of innovation. In 2009, when real unemployment was 16.7 percent and rising, the president said, "Innovation has been essential to our prosperity in the past, and it will be essential to our prosperity in the future."[1] Gary Locke, Obama's former commerce secretary and current envoy to China, said, "Innovation and entrepreneurship fuel America's economy. It's what enables our businesses to grow, create new products and services, and generate new jobs."[2]

"Ultimately, to create manufacturing jobs, we've got to be innovating," says General Electric CEO Jeffrey Immelt.[3] On the other hand, Larry Summers, who served as one of Obama's closest economic advisers, has said, "America's role is to feed a global economy that's increasingly based on knowledge and services rather than on making stuff."[4] And Gary Shapiro, the president and CEO of the Consumer Electronics Association, says flatly, "Innovation, not manufacturing, will bring jobs."[5]

So which is it? Can the United States be an innovator without manufacturing? Or do the two go hand in hand? Is it enough for the United States to focus on building a knowledge economy that fosters innovation?

No. Sorry, but innovation alone is worth nothing. Platitudes about innovation are worth even less. As solutions go, if you think innovation is going to save us, you're dreaming. You simply can't sustain a diverse, vibrant, large-scale economy like that of the United States on innovation alone. Look, there are no magic bullets. Not all innovation translates into jobs. Not by a long shot.

Two basic facts tell the story. In the past decade, about 6 million manufacturing jobs have disappeared.[6] In the meantime, jobs in so-called innovative industries—information technology, telecom, electronics, and professional and technical services—have remained pretty much flat. While everyone may *say* innovation is the wave of the future, the jobs have not followed from the rhetoric.

If we've learned anything from long experience on this great big planet of ours, it's that everything is interrelated. Innovation is an important part of being successful as a company and as a country. Innovation is a big part of all that—but it isn't the only part.

Why do I say that? Perfect example: The United States spends billions of dollars in research and development for new technologies and

FIGURE 6.1   JOBS IN INNOVATIVE INDUSTRIES COMPARED TO MANUFACTURING

The United States has not seen any job growth in innovative industries while 5.3 million manufacturing jobs have disappeared since 2000

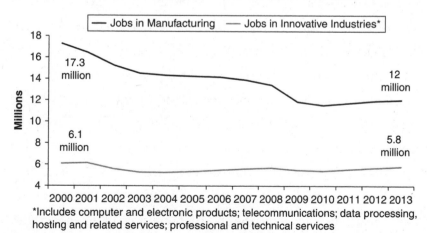

*Includes computer and electronic products; telecommunications; data processing, hosting and related services; professional and technical services

Source: *Bureau of Labor Statistics, Current Employment Statistics, http://www.bls .gov/ces/.*

new processes—about $400 billion in 2009.[7] That's still the highest in the world, although China, Russia, and the European Union are catching up fast. Who's doing that research? Universities, certainly, with sizable backing from the federal government. And think about the hundreds of billions that the federal government has spent over the years on defense research.

The Defense Advanced Research Projects Agency is one of the great legacies of the Sputnik crisis. DARPA has had a hand in artificial intelligence research, supersonic and stealth flight, passive radar, the driverless car, and creation of a certain computer network that eventually became the Internet. But a large percentage of R&D spending today comes from the private manufacturing sector.

You need to be able to make and use what you innovate. You cannot expect to reap the real benefits of innovation if you leave the making and the building to other countries. If you innovate a new product, a process, or a technology in the United States, but don't make it here, you are essentially spitting in the ocean of innovation. And sooner rather than later you will lose your ability to innovate, because the driving force behind the need will have disappeared from your shores.

Suppose you invent a new solar panel, a new memory chip, or maybe a device that revolutionizes the way millions of people read books and magazines. But you decide you can't make your product in the United States. It's too expensive. There are too many regulations. You can't hire enough qualified workers. Whatever. So you make it in China to save on costs. The Chinese welcome your business and won't burden you with a lot of rules—at least none that you need to worry about right away. And, by the way, the Chinese are only too happy to reap the technical benefits of your innovation, even as they feed you subsidies and tax breaks and manipulated currency.

It's a remarkable fact that we invent new technology in the United States, contract with Asian manufacturing plants, and ship components to China for assembly. Then China exports the technology to the United States, further exacerbating the U.S. trade deficit even though it's our own technology that we're importing.

To illustrate, consider the success of Amazon.com's e-reader-turned-tablet computer, the Kindle. Amazon has enjoyed enormous success with the Kindle family, selling more than 8 million of the tablets and dominating a market that barely existed five years ago.[8] Amazon conceived the device in Seattle and developed the e-reader in the United States. But it is manufactured almost entirely overseas, with segments of production in at least five different countries, including the United States.

The bottom line: of the $180 Amazon spends to make one of its e-readers, only $45 is captured in the United States. Roughly the same is true of Apple's iPhone, Barnes & Noble's Nook, and any number of gadgets that Silicon Valley has invented and subsequently outsourced to Asia.

Even more remarkable is how American companies are being robbed blind of their patented inventions and trade secrets. China doesn't respect intellectual property the way we do, or the way most other countries do. Software, movie, and music piracy is rampant in China. Not only that, Chinese nationals will often steal trade secrets from U.S. firms and sell them to Chinese companies. Fact: in 2010, the U.S. International Trade Commission banned imports of railroad

FIGURE 6.2   HOW THE KINDLE ADDS TO THE US TRADE DEFICIT

Of the Kindle's $180 in manufacturing costs, only $45 is
captured in the United States.

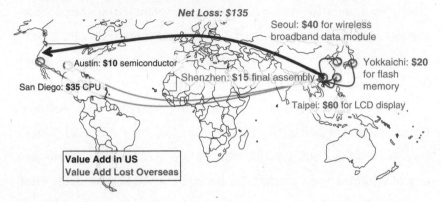

Source: *Willy Shih, "The U.S. Can't Manufacture the Kindle and That's a Problem,"*
Harvard Business Review, *October 13, 2009, http://blogs.hbr.org/2009/10/the-us
-cant-manufacture-the-ki/.*

parts from Tianrui, a Chinese steel fabricator, after they began making
the same parts as Chicago's Amsted Industries using Amsted's secret
process without a license. They did it by hiring away nine workers—
eight of whom signed a confidentiality agreement and all of whom
were informed not to disclose the secrets of the process—from another
Chinese company (Datong) who licensed the production process from
Amsted.

Anybody doing business in China knows this sort of stuff is going
on all the time. They complain. We demand that Chinese authorities

do something about it. And the Chinese promise to crack down. They promise better patent and copyright protection. They promise to help guard trade secrets. Lots of promises, little action. If the United States had a vibrant manufacturing sector, intellectual property issues wouldn't be such a big deal.

Despite knowing the risks, companies will relocate their research and development overseas because companies will realize that if it's cheaper or more convenient to manufacture overseas, it's probably easier to innovate overseas, too.

It's already happening. Many Fortune 500 companies are moving their research labs to China, and they've poured billions of dollars into R&D facilities overseas in the past five years. Why? Why would they do that? That's just the way it works. Where you invent, you build. Where you build, you invent. That's Mother Nature and the human mind and the human process doing what they've always done. So to simply say "We've got to be innovators" misses the point if we don't also recognize we need to make what we innovate. Otherwise we lose everything.

I'm not against other countries doing the same thing, by the way. In fact, most countries do exactly what I'm talking about. That's how great trade and industrial policies are made. But if you lack a core, all the rest is just rhetoric divorced from the reality of how the world works. What I'm suggesting here is a view of the world that believes we can succeed not in spite of hard reality but because of it. It's a vision that's optimistic, that believes our problems can be solved, and that human beings, with all of their ingenuity, inventiveness, and natural desire for improvement, can succeed. But it requires balance.

THE SKILLS GAP MYTH

So innovation alone isn't going to get us out of the crisis. But how can the United States put millions of people to work when the United States is apparently suffering from a crippling lack of skills? The National Association of Manufacturers estimates there are about 600,000 jobs that have gone unfilled for lack of applicants with the right sets of skills.[9]

President Obama attempted to address the question in his 2012 State of the Union Address. "I . . . hear from many business leaders who want to hire in the United States but can't find workers with the right skills," the president said. "Growing industries in science and technology have twice as many openings as we have workers who can do the job."[10]

Mitt Romney also made the skills gap a political campaign issue. "We have millions of jobs that are open that can't be filled because people don't have the skills they need for those jobs," he said on the campaign trail in Ohio just after Labor Day.[11]

I disagree. Just as innovation is the great false hope for saving the country, the skills gap is greatly exaggerated. Technology changes; processes change. People's skills become outmoded; people pick up new skills. Workers coming into the workforce have got the newer skills; those leaving the workforce don't have them; and the people that are still in the workforce have to learn and keep up.

Are Americans suddenly incapable? No, of course not. The problem is we've allowed distortions to take place that encourage companies to make some counterproductive and self-destructive decisions.

If you want to get people back to work, don't complain to me about a skills shortage. That's an excuse. Here's the truth: we have a skills shortage every decade, in both good times and bad. Heck, we have a skills shortage every few years.

We should ask ourselves, what were 8 million people doing before the economy collapsed in 2008? They were all gainfully employed, with skills they already had. Those skills haven't suddenly gone away. When employers talk about the skills gap, what do they mean? A 2012 survey by McKinsey and Company found that only 42 percent of employers think new graduates are "adequately prepared" to enter the workforce.[12] Many of those employers are looking for candidates with experience already, and a growing number of companies surveyed say they are reluctant to hire anyone but candidates that fit a peculiar or vague set of job requirements. That's why you often see newspaper stories about thousands of people applying for a few jobs only to find they aren't "qualified." Other employers, when asked, will say they can find plenty of qualified people, but very few willing to take the wages being offered. That isn't a skills gap, but rather a market gap.

But the problem is made worse by a lack of mobility. Millions of people can't sell their homes because the burst housing bubble left their mortgages deeply underwater. They're stuck in a house they couldn't afford and they can't sell, or they're rooted for other reasons. There may be jobs in Texas or North Dakota, where a welder or an electrician today can make $80,000 a year working on an oil rig. But millions of Americans are staying where they are and have no plans to move, even if they have the right skills. They can't afford to.

FIGURE 6.3   AREAS HIT HARDEST BY THE GREAT RECESSION

While the national unemployment rate continues to fall,
localized rates vary widely

Unemployment Rate by County (July 2012–June 2013)

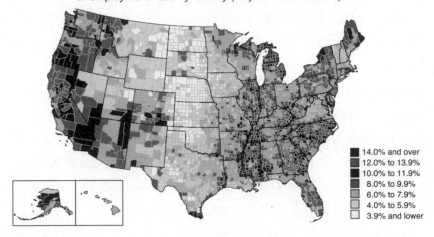

14.0% and over
12.0% to 13.9%
10.0% to 11.9%
8.0% to 9.9%
6.0% to 7.9%
4.0% to 5.9%
3.9% and lower

Source: *Bureau of Labor Statistics, Local Area Unemployment, http://www.bls.gov
/lau/.*

Sometimes I think that a lot of companies are just lazy. When I hear
a CEO talking about the lack of qualified American workers, I always
ask, "When you moved to China, what were the skill sets over there?" I
can tell you the answer: There weren't any. All of these companies had
to take people and train them. But they didn't squawk about it because
the process was totally pain-free. China—and Singapore, and Korea,
and Vietnam, and so on—offered them all kinds of government incentives that made it profitable for them to move there.

Why don't we do that here? We need policies that make it profitable for companies to come back here, to go through that training pain and development, and, at the end of the day, have a significant profit opportunity when they're done.

Now, I know the objection: we have lots and lots of taxpayer-funded job-training programs in this country. Most of the job-training programs we have are terrible. Most of them only last a few months, and all they do is teach people how to write a passable résumé or how to get along in the workplace. They don't really offer credentials in specific fields. Most of these programs don't even work with employers. Why in the world would you spend time and money "training" people for jobs the local economy might not ever need?

The situation in the United States may be worse than it should be because Congress and the president haven't put in place good policies that would give employers and workers incentives to get the training they need. We know what kind of skills and training we need to rebuild a healthy economy. Instead of addressing the normal skills gap that develops over time, we're practically encouraging wanton neglect. And on top of that, we've got shortages of the workers with the most valuable skill sets in the geographical regions where we need them most.

Complaining about it won't do a damn thing. The situation isn't going to change overnight. We've got to create an environment that encourages universities and schools to create the programs that generate the necessary skills, because there will be jobs for those people when they graduate.

THE RIGHT KIND OF EDUCATION AND TRAINING

In the United States today, the prevailing view is that everyone should get a four-year college degree and that manufacturing work is the realm of the uneducated high school dropout, the sort of person lacking other career prospects. That's a mistake. Skilled electricians, truck drivers, welders, and carpenters can make excellent money in North Dakota's oil fields right now, while people with bachelor's degrees in English or sociology are waiting tables or answering phones for minimum wage. According to the Bureau of Labor Statistics, there are about 5,000 janitors in the United States with PhDs.[13]

It's insane. We're spending $500 billion a year in this country—federal, state, and local—on public education. Where do those resources go? I don't think we need more janitors with doctorates. I think we need more workers with certificates in computer programming and industrial design. Should Americans expect the public schools to train workers in the skills they supposedly need when a business may not know from month to month, or year to year, what those skills will be? Governments have a vital role to play. But businesses need to step up and take some initiative. Do your homework, go get the people who can be trained, and train them.

Our public education system is not geared toward creating the skills businesses say they want because they haven't been in demand. Instead, they've been demeaned. What parent is going to encourage their kid to become an engineer or a welder or an electrician if they think there are no jobs for them? So you put them into liberal arts, and when they graduate they can't do squat. That's a failure of our whole system, and it's not something that can be reversed overnight.

So why not say that the United States intends to rebuild its manufacturing sector, and that we're going to need more engineers, more programmers, more people with the technical know-how to work and thrive in a modern manufacturing environment? The market will respond, if we let it. Eventually, people in the schools will say, "If I want more funding, I'd better do the stuff that the businesses want done and that the steel guys want done and the computer techs want done."

The market will provide. There's going to be a time lag, no doubt, but the market will provide. Build it, and they will come. Don't build it, and they won't come.

You're not going to get instant gratification from government. That isn't how government works. Manufacturers need to fill the breach. We need to take on the responsibility to keep our workforce skill sets current. It's our job to get the right people trained to the level we need them to be. We can't expect government to do everything. We can make partnerships, we can work with state and local governments to help develop the tools and the curricula we need. But we can't expect to be China, where the government does it all—or at least, we shouldn't.

We need to set reasonable expectations about the role of public education. Basic skills should come early. Currently, about 2 million college students spend part of their first year in higher education relearning skills they should have mastered in high school or earlier. A 2012 study by ACT, Inc., a company that gives an alternative to the SAT college readiness test, found that most high school seniors fail benchmark standards for science and math. The picture was only a little better in reading and writing. If we're failing to deliver basic skills in the elementary grades, we're going to lag in advanced skills. You could spend a fortune expecting to get from point A to point B, but you'll never get there if you don't know how to use a compass. So we need to get the basics right.

But let's acknowledge what an education is really for. Obviously, you have trade schools and professional schools that teach people what they need to know in a real world setting. But school is mostly about giving you the confidence to know that you can learn whatever you have to learn out there. Learning is a lifelong endeavor. School is important while it lasts, but if you stop learning the day you leave, you don't stay in the workforce very long—or get too far.

The most important thing people learn in school is how to learn. What did I know about thermodynamics before I picked up a book? What did I know about calculus? What did I know about American history? Not a damn thing. But I went to school and I learned. The point is to instill a degree of confidence that you can learn whatever it is you have to learn to be a success in this world—that's what education's all about.

I think back to when I was a kid growing up in the 1960s, trying to figure out where I wanted to go and what I wanted to do with my life. When the country was focused on resolving a particular crisis and reaching a certain goal—reaching the moon, beating the Soviets—we had real purpose in our education system. My guidance counselors saw that I had an aptitude for math and science and pushed me in that direction. My parents encouraged me, too. We need something like that today. If we want to restore our prominence in manufacturing and re-build a strong middle class, then our education system should be reori-ented toward those goals.

The education system shouldn't extol careers that do little except generate phony wealth or mean a lifetime of low-paid service work. We don't need more high-finance guys or social workers. We need to instead let the next generation know there are good, well-paying jobs waiting for them in hands-on work where they can create, make, and build things. Let's put an aptitude for math and science together with the right education to develop the necessary skills to do the jobs that we are going to create.

President Obama has made a point of promoting college degrees for everyone. "I've always believed that we should be doing everything we can to help put higher education within reach for every single American student—because the unemployment rate for Americans with at least a college degree is about half the national average," he told an audience of college students in April 2012. Should more Americans get a bach-elor degree? What should U.S. higher education look like? We shouldn't limit higher education to just four-year liberal arts degrees. We need a lot more vocational and technical training options.

At Nucor, we work with local vocational-technical centers and pro-vide financial support so they have the means to train students in how to weld, how to be electricians, how to program computers, how to be a mechanic—really, how to develop multiple skill sets, because in manu-facturing it's not all pushbuttons. We tend to put more emphasis on electronics, but we also need people who can use sledgehammers and crowbars, too. We also work closely with community colleges to put industrial engineering programs in place. Those programs are really for students who are coming out of high school who don't know what they want to do but who have a natural aptitude for the work.

The truth is, most kids don't know what the heck they want to do when they grow up. I had an aptitude, so I kept moving in a direction that took advantage of that aptitude, even when I had no idea where it would land me. We need to extend those same sorts of advantages to students today, which is why industry should take a more aggressive role in education.

As for government's part in all of this, beyond the role the feds and states play in funding colleges and universities, the best thing it could do is create a regulatory environment in which manufacturers can build plants and actually create the need for the skills we should be teaching.

If we really want to get students excited, let's put them in the real working world. I can tell you that at Nucor, we haven't been complaining about any skills gap. We're not going into community colleges or local universities and asking why they don't have an industrial engineering degree program. If the community college doesn't have one, we'll help with funding to get the program started. In fact, we're traveling the United States, telling any college administrator who will listen that we want to assist in any way we can to put those programs in place.

We also reach out to college students studying civil engineering or metallurgical engineering. We're looking for leaders for tomorrow. We want those students. We want them to come to our mills to see exactly what it is we do every day, and to learn what it takes to be part of a steelmaking operation. Those students, we hope, are going to eventually move into leadership roles in the company—supervisor, department manager, general manager of a plant. One of them might be CEO someday.

We've got recruiters going out to universities. We're working with a dozen or more to develop relationships and attract freshmen and sophomores into our companywide internship program at our plants all over the country, where we give them real work to do from day one. And they go back to school and share stories about what great experiences they had. We even send our employees to elementary schools to talk about what it's like to work in a steel mill, what kinds of jobs are available, why they're exciting, what kind of money they make.

We have the jobs; we need you to put programs in place to train people with the necessary skills—or at least the aptitude to learn those skills.

As U.S. manufacturing has declined, many manufacturers have abandoned apprenticeship and internship programs. Nucor has bucked the trend with a robust internship program, with some 200 interns around the company. Many of those interns are eligible to receive scholarships from the Nucor Foundation. It's a paid program, and, as with all of our teammates, we aren't going to pay interns something for nothing. And we don't just ignore them. We keep track of them. We want to make sure their experiences are positive, that they do things that get them excited, learn about what their capabilities are, and get stressed out a little bit. Many of them go on to become full-time members of the team. We're running these programs across the country because we recognize it's an investment in the future.

Other companies are making similar investments. Boeing, for example, has developed an online training program in partnership with

Edmonds Community College near its Washington state headquarters. The program is aimed at retraining workers to meet the company's specific manufacturing needs. About 75 percent of the program's graduates go on to work for the aerospace company full time.[14]

John Deere sponsors a program at Southeast Community College in Nebraska, where the company provides trucks and tractors to train technicians and will pay students' tuition if they agree to work for a certain period in John Deere dealerships. Ford and General Motors fund similar programs in auto technology around the Midwest.

One objection to corporate-backed programs at public community colleges is that companies are essentially financing their job-training programs with tax dollars. The claim is that these companies stand to benefit more than the public does. From time to time, I'll hear objections to the partnerships Nucor makes with colleges and universities, or I'll read complaints about the kind of vocational training that John Deere and Boeing are trying to do in community colleges. The gist of these complaints is that I'm a CEO from a big manufacturing company trying to get the public to train my future employees for free.

I don't see it that way at all. I'm an American. I've believed in the American system of free markets—warts and all—all my life. Now, I happen to work in a very basic industry. If the economy is doing well, most times our business does well; if the economy is not doing well, we don't do well. We see the pain. We get hit first. Those of us in the steel industry are in a unique position to see all of the distortions in the U.S. economy. Whether it's the distortions in our international trading system or the distortions in domestic regulations, they hit us first and they impact us daily. The same is true of the distortions in our education system and our so-called innovation economy.

The United States is at a crossroads now. People are starting to see that things need to be done differently. The economic crisis exposed systemic failures that few people even knew existed. Hundreds of thousands of students are leaving college every year looking for useful work fit for their educational level. Instead, they're flipping hamburgers or sitting at home playing video games all day. And we're wasting a lot of money and education on people who will need to be retrained in some skill set in order to be successful. What we're doing now isn't working. What works is creating an environment that links innovation with the manufacturing sector and creates jobs for the skills our workforce already has.

Our first priority should be putting people back to work by focusing on the areas where people lost their jobs. This is not rocket science; this is common sense. So if you've lost jobs for people with construction or manufacturing skills, what do you do? You certainly don't send them to school to become data-entry specialists or grocery clerks. The manufacturing sector is well positioned to help the U.S. economy create jobs. Even though manufacturing has suffered greatly over the past decade, there are a few bright spots. The automotive industry has experienced a nice comeback. Tech companies such as Apple, embarrassed by inhumane working conditions in their factories overseas, are promising to return at least some of their manufacturing to the United States. What hasn't come back, and what continues to drag down economic recovery, is construction.

We're not building things that need to be built and we're not examining where we could spend the money most efficiently to create jobs. We have a glaring need for infrastructure; it's staring us right in the face. Our infrastructure is crumbling. We need $3.6 trillion of infrastructure work over the next five to six years. If we're going to be globally competitive again, we need a sound infrastructure. We're so far behind it's ridiculous. Everybody knows it.

I'm not talking about "bridges to nowhere." I'm not talking about copying the Chinese and building massive new cities that sit empty, just because their construction workers needed something to do. I'm talking about roads, highways, bridges, dams, canals, levies, communications lines, power grids—real projects, real needs. Think of it this way: in mid-2014, more than 710,000 construction workers sat idle. At the peak of the housing bubble, 7.7 million Americans worked in construction. Today, it's only 6 million.[15] With an annual infrastructure shortfall of $201 billion over the next eight years,[16] that's 2 million additional construction jobs.[17] Two million Americans who could be working well-paying jobs.

To meet those needs, we're going to have to spend some money. We don't like the idea that we're in debt, but this is the kind of spending that's going to have a bigger return than the dollars we're spending. It's going to take a few years. Nothing's going to turn this situation around overnight. But, as with most everything in life, we need a balanced, self-supporting, and dynamic approach.

SEVEN

MORE MYTHS THAT DISTRACT US

And What to Do about Them

THE VAST MAJORITY OF AMERICANS—DEMOCRATS, Republicans, and independents alike—think the federal government spends too much money. Anyone can see that Congress spends more money than the treasury takes in. As of October 2014, the United States had a $483 billion budget deficit[1] and more than $17.9 trillion in national debt.[2] A poll taken just before the 2010 midterm elections by the Tarrance Group and Hart Research found that more than two-thirds of likely voters believe excessive government spending hurts the country and their personal finances.[3]

It's a problem. Not the greatest problem we face, but people worry. I think what most people don't understand is that government policy hurts growth and makes the jobs crisis worse not by spending too much money, but by spending on the wrong things in the wrong way. Focusing on "how much" instead of "how" and "where" is a mistake.

Think back to the stimulus debate in 2009. I think most Americans understand that the nearly $1 trillion plan that Congress and President Obama passed didn't work as promised. Adjusted for inflation, the American Recovery and Reinvestment Act was bigger than the New Deal's Works Progress Administration, which was supposed to help end the Great Depression. It was bigger than the Marshall Plan, which helped rebuild Europe and contain Soviet communism after World War II. All told, the federal government spent about five times as much on the 2009 stimulus as we spent to put Neil Armstrong on the moon in 1969.[4]

Does anyone really think the stimulus was money well spent? No way. Not even close. But, remember, I supported the stimulus plan. I hated to ask the government to do anything for us. But we had no choice. The crisis was unprecedented. Something had to be done, and the government was in the ideal position to do it. When the credit crisis hit, it was immediate—like dominoes falling, one after the other. No one had ever seen anything like it. The private sector was in a tailspin. Customers simply vanished, because they couldn't get the financing they needed. With no credit, construction just stopped. It was like somebody suddenly turned off a water spigot.

The crisis cut our business in half, and our people were really hurting. Nucor didn't lay anybody off, but everyone in the company took a pay cut. During the very worst days of the crisis, our teammates were making 50 percent of their usual pay.

I thought a well-designed stimulus might have done a lot of good under the circumstances. That's why I talked up the "Buy American" language in the law, to make sure the stimulus money stayed in the United States. I'm not a union guy, but that time I was on the same side as Richard Trumka of the AFL-CIO. It was absolutely the right thing to do. I said then, and I still say, that if we wanted to stimulate our economy, we needed to spend our tax dollars on U.S. products and services.

Yes, "Buy American" would have benefited the steel industry. So what? The purpose of the stimulus, and it was the right purpose, was to stop the bleeding of jobs and to create new jobs here in America. Not overseas. Not in China or India or Europe. The point was to benefit the whole U.S. economic engine.

Ultimately, Congress passed and President Obama signed a bill stipulating that stimulus funds could only go for American-made steel, unless such purchases violated U.S.-trade agreements. That allowed Canadian and European steel in, but kept cheaper, subsidized Chinese and Russian steel out.

The goal of the "Buy American" provision was to avoid a situation similar to one surrounding the San Francisco–Oakland Bay Bridge reconstruction project following the 1989 Loma Prieta earthquake. Millions of people watched the quake happen on live TV, just as the third game of the World Series was about to get underway. The 6.9 quake caused widespread damage and collapsed part of the double-deck Bay Bridge, killing one driver. Although the bridge reopened about six weeks later, state transportation officials knew the bridge needed to be upgraded or replaced. In 1994, California's Department of Transportation estimated that retrofitting the bridge would cost $230 million.

California officials eventually decided to replace the bridge altogether. In 1996, the estimated cost of replacement was $1 billion. Six more years would pass before all of the environmental impact studies were finished and permits obtained. The job was supposed to be done by 2007. Now, the new Bay Bridge opened on Labor Day in 2013 at a cost of more than $7.2 billion, not including interest on the bonds the state floated to finance construction.[5] What happened?

California got the idea they could save money and speed up construction by putting the bridge's steel work out to bid internationally. Not only that, they said they had no choice. The man in charge of California's bridge program went on television and said the largest companies in America didn't have the capacity to do the work on a tight schedule.[6] I think that's baloney. We could have built it several times over!

Here's what really happened. California had its own "Buy American" language, which Arnold Schwarzenegger dumped a few months after he became governor in 2003. A group of U.S. steelmakers were all set to bid on the project. They planned to construct a new fabricating plant in the Pacific Northwest. It would have created thousands of jobs for American workers. Instead, California awarded a $1.4 billion contract to American Bridge, which promptly subcontracted with a company in Shanghai. The Chinese company did all of the major work.

You might say, "Oh, well. The Americans got underbid by a foreign competitor. That's the free market for you." Wrong. It isn't a free market when China can undercut American manufacturers with manipulated currency, subsidies, and cheap labor.

The topper, though, is the Bay Bridge project opened six years late and California's taxpayers spent hundreds of millions of dollars more than the state transportation department initially estimated, all with the promise of saving money. All they did was help create thousands of jobs in China. As it turns out, cheap can be pretty expensive.

U.S. policy makers learned little from the California experience. Even with watered-down "Buy American" language in the law, the 2009 stimulus package was a huge disappointment for a lot of reasons. The big one was that the money Americans got from it went principally to buy foreign-made goods.

So the stimulus didn't develop what economists call the "multiplier effect" to create jobs domestically. When economic activity goes up— as in the case of government spending money on public works—it's supposed to create a chain reaction, with one dollar of spending generating more than one dollar of growth as the money spreads. Infrastructure has the greatest multiplier effects, the most job-creation potential, and the most economic impact compared to other types of spending. According to Moody's, every dollar we spend on infrastructure boosts GDP by $1.59.[7]

We didn't spread the money around in the right places, and we let too much money go abroad, so we got no bang for the buck. The Chinese did. When *we* went into the 2008 crisis, *they* spent $750 billion on infrastructure alone. What did we do? We planned to put $60 billion of the $800 billion stimulus into infrastructure spending. And then only half of that got spent, because the states didn't have the money to match it.

But almost every dollar that Congress gave back to the American people came in the way of temporary tax breaks or rebates. What purpose did that serve? Apart from giving politicians something to claim credit for, about 80 percent of that money got spent on products and services coming from abroad. That's where our wealth—borrowed wealth, for the most part—ended up. It didn't go to creating jobs here, except on the periphery. And the one place Congress could have put those billions that would have had a positive multiplier effect, they settled on a piddling $30 billion. To put the number in perspective, $30 billion would barely cover the necessary upgrades and repairs to bridges, roads, and highways in Southern California. Another $30 billion would take care of Northern California's roads and waterways.

An aging infrastructure is a drag on economic growth. By one estimate, traffic congestion and freight delays cost the country $200 billion a year.[8] Potholed roads cost commuters $67 billion a year in repairs and other operating costs.[9] Americans spend 4.2 billion hours every year idling in traffic.[10] In addition, the Federal Highway Administration says nearly 8,000 U.S. bridges are either "structurally deficient" or "fracture critical."[11] A "structurally deficient" bridge has one or two defects. A "fracture critical" bridge has nothing to hold it up if something fails, as happened in 2007 with the I-35W Mississippi River Bridge in Minneapolis. The rush hour disaster killed 13 people and injured 145 more. Most estimates put the cost of repairing the nation's most dangerous bridges somewhere between $30 billion and $60 billion.[12]

Improving infrastructure should be a no-brainer. We've got a priority, right? We've got to get our economy going again. But we have two problems. The first is a major degradation of the infrastructure we already have. The second is figuring out the new infrastructure we need. The foundation is crumbling, but we also need a modern, technology-enabled version of the old models. So we're talking about rebuilding and strengthening the backbone of our economy, but we're also talking about ways to make our infrastructure more efficient. It's not just steel and concrete and asphalt. It's fiber-optic cable, wireless networks, and satellite technology. As bad as some of our roads and bridges are, our telecommunications infrastructure needs a major overhaul, too. And don't forget the air-traffic control system. What we have now is like a rope bridge instead of a steel structure. And the United States lags most of the world in high-speed Internet access. Fact: according to the Organization for Economic Co-operation and Development, 70 percent of Americans have access to high-speed connections, compared with 94 percent of South Koreans. And the average connection speed in Seoul is about 200 times faster than it is in Charlotte.[13]

Don't forget, a road is a road is a road. We may figure out better ways of collecting tolls, or invent sophisticated ways of sequencing traffic patterns to ease congestion, or even perfect a driverless car. But we still need roads and bridges for all of it. And by the way, once we do that, the benefits extend to the whole world, not just the United States, because foreign investors will be more likely to put their money into a country that offers an excellent infrastructure and the rule of law, enforceable contracts, robust protections for intellectual and private property, and capitalism rightly understood. But as long as we're in this funk, we're not helping the world and we're sure as hell not helping ourselves.

HOW TO THINK ABOUT GOVERNMENT SPENDING

The American Society of Civil Engineers estimates the United States would need to invest $3.6 trillion in new infrastructure spending by 2020 in order raise the nation's bridges, roads, dams, waterways, and levees to a "B" grade. Currently, the ASCE gives U.S. infrastructure a "D+" grade overall.[14] But there is little movement in Washington, D.C., or in the states to provide additional funding for infrastructure improvements. The political fight in Congress is centered on deficit and debt reduction and curtailing wasteful spending. Why is that wrong?

Again, I happen to agree with Rahm Emanuel that a crisis is a terrible thing to waste. But it's important to define what *waste* means. There is a right way to take advantage of a crisis: to bring people together, to focus on what really needs to be done to undo economic problems and distortions that were decades in the making. Our political leadership had that golden opportunity in 2009. And we all know what happened instead: most everyone in Washington, from the president on down, saw an opportunity to get everything they couldn't get when Bill Clinton and George W. Bush were in the White House.

The irony is that if we do the right things first, we'll be much better positioned to address *everyone's* public policy wish lists. You want green jobs? You want universal health care? If we had a growing economy, we'd have more tax revenues and more money to pay for all of those things.

This sounds like an oversimplification, but it really isn't. The reason spending is so out of control, and why the Chinese have been so happy to buy trillions of dollars' worth of U.S. treasuries, is that we've created an economic system that's not creating real wealth. Trust me, very few people would be complaining about spending $1 trillion on health-care reform over the next decade—or much of anything else for that matter—if we had the actual revenue to pay for it all.

Republicans and Democrats need to get their priorities straight. Republicans are in austerity mode. You saw it with the debt ceiling fight in 2011, and you saw it again with the fiscal cliff debacle after the 2012 election. Republicans say, "Hey, we're broke. We don't have the revenue. We've got to stop spending." Well, sorry, we can't simply stop spending. And we shouldn't. The old business saying also happens to be true of government: it takes money to make money. It's important to get the revenue going so we can spend without bankrupting ourselves.

The only way to overcome our fiscal woes is to grow out of the problem. Simply settling for 2 percent GDP growth and 150,000 new jobs a month isn't going to cut it. Don't buy into the "new normal" rhetoric. This isn't at all controversial, or at least it shouldn't be. There was a time, not so very long ago, when every Republican and every Democrat agreed with that idea. It's just common sense. If we met our infrastructure needs, that would generate growth and create millions of jobs. And say what you want about the Federal Reserve's monetary policies, but right now the money is basically free. Interest rates are low, and are likely to remain so as long as unemployment remains near 6 percent.

What I'm advocating is *investment*. It's not spending. If the government focused on a few guarantees and was open to bringing the private sector into these projects and making sure the regulations are reasonable so everyone is protected, it would be a tremendous win. I can't stress this enough. From a business standpoint, you have operating expenses and capital expenses. Operating expenses are the year-to-year, month-to-month, day-to-day costs of doing business. Capital expenses are investments in things like equipment and machinery and new facilities. Those are big expenses, but they pay dividends over the long run.

Straightforward, long-term solutions aren't always conducive to getting people re-elected. They don't play well in a two-year election cycle or a four-year election cycle, where short-term thinking rules. The trouble with a short-term mentality is that it creates long-term problems. These problems are only going to get more expensive the longer we wait. So civil engineers said we had a $3 trillion infrastructure problem in 2012.[15] In 2013, it's $3.6 trillion.[16] Next year, it will be $4 trillion. What's it going to be the year after that? It takes a strong leader with strong communication skills and passion to be able to sell the American people on what needs to be done.

Most Americans will buy into those solutions because they know right from wrong. Most Americans know the difference between frivolous and productive spending. We also know that in order to be able to pay back our debts, we've got to make more money than we're spending. We've got to create economic growth that lets us pay back the loans we took out from the Chinese, the Japanese, the Saudis—and from ourselves. But in a low-growth or no-growth economy, you can't do that.

STIMULUS AND THE GREEN JOBS MYTH

The 2009 stimulus should have focused on proven ways to create jobs. Instead, Congress and the president spent billions on other ways of re-inventing the economy, such as clean energy and green jobs. So while Congress allocated about $60 billion for infrastructure, and spent about half of that money, lawmakers also put nearly $100 billion into green initiatives.

Though I'm convinced that money was largely wasted, the agenda wasn't the least bit surprising. When Barack Obama first ran for president in 2008, he promised to "transform" America's economy by creating millions of green jobs. When he stood on stage in Denver at the climax of the 2008 Democratic National Convention, Obama promised he would invest $150 billion over the next decade in "affordable, renewable sources of energy—wind power and solar power and the next generation of biofuels; an investment that will lead to new industries and 5 million new jobs that pay well and can't ever be outsourced."[17] The new green economy, Obama said, would be an "engine of economic growth" that would outdo the information technology revolution.[18]

I don't mean to come off as a spoilsport here, but we didn't need a "transformation." We needed a recovery. Green jobs and clean energy weren't the areas of the U.S. economy we needed to jumpstart in the midst of an unprecedented crisis. Now, I know Obama wasn't the only candidate talking about that. John McCain did, too. Green technology had fairly broad bipartisan appeal. Arnold Schwarzenegger constantly talked about green energy and green jobs when he was governor of California. His successor, Jerry Brown, is also a big cheerleader for clean energy and green jobs. Around the country, you can find plenty of Democrats and Republicans talking about the need for high-tech solutions to our economic woes.

Since 2009, the federal government has spent $400 million in green jobs training. Most of that money went to states in the form of grants. The U.S. Department of Labor's inspector general audited the program in 2012 and found that most of the money was wasted on useless retraining of employed workers, and only 38 percent of workers who completed the training programs found jobs. Of those, only 16 percent stayed employed longer than six months.[19]

Federal spending created just 9,245 new jobs in "green tech" by the end of 2011, according to Labor Department figures.[20] In some cases, the jobs cost exponentially more to create than they paid in salary. The National Renewable Energy Laboratory (NREL) found that $9 billion in stimulus funds that went to solar and wind projects between 2009 and 2011 created just 910 "direct" jobs.[21] That works out to $9.89 million per job. When NREL included the 4,600 or so "indirect" jobs associated with those projects, the cost dropped to $1.6 million per job. The Department of Energy disputes the Labor Department figure, estimating that the stimulus was responsible for creating upward of 82,000 green jobs since 2009.[22] During the same period, certain green sectors lost jobs. The American Wind Energy Association, for example, says the windmill manufacturing business has shed 10,000 jobs over the past four years.[23]

All of those jobs the Energy Department brags about—where exactly were they created? As I understand it, the federal government admits that as much as 80 percent of the stimulus—with something on order of $2.3 billion in tax credits for green-tech companies—went to South Korea, Germany, Spain, and, of course, China.[24] If we're trying to get out of a hole and create 30 million new jobs, that isn't helpful.

I think there is a lot of fudging when it comes to green jobs, specifically what they are and how many of them we can expect to create. One of the most damning charts I've ever seen from the Bureau of Labor Statistics breaks down some of the jobs the feds consider green. These include—no joke—carbon emissions allowance traders on Wall Street, bus drivers, insulation installers, and environmental photographers. By that standard, we could reclassify Nucor's steel workers as green, because our company is the largest scrap recycler in the country and we're always finding ways to make our processes more efficient and less

FIGURE 7.1 DEFINITIONS OF "GREEN JOBS"

A wide variety of sectors claim to create green jobs, although their "greenness" is often questionable

Industries with Green Jobs	
Sector	Example
Recycled material merchant wholesalers	Wholesalers of scrap materials (i.e., Nucor)
Securities and commodity exchanges	Emissions allowance trading
Public relations agencies	Environmental advertising or public awareness
Contractors	Construction of LEED-eligible buildings
Travel agencies	Ecotourism
Computer programmers	Energy usage specialists
Newspapers, television, and other news media	Environmental content for news media
Museums	Environmental and science museums
Charter bus industry	Multipassenger commuter services

Source: *"Industries Where Green Goods and Services Are Classified," Bureau of Labor Statistics, August 24, 2010, http://www.bls.gov/green/final_green_def _8242010_pub.pdf.*

carbon intensive. But I somehow doubt our environmentalist friends would go for that, although they should.

Sunil Sharan, the former director of General Electric's Smart Grid Initiative, wrote in the *Washington Post* in 2010 that the belief that green jobs could make a serious dent in the U.S. unemployment rate was always far-fetched. Sharan noted how the Obama administration allocated a little over $4 billion in stimulus money to building the smart grid, which is an important piece of infrastructure for our future. The plan was to install 20 million "smart meters" over five years. Smart meters are simply digital versions of the old spinning electric meter. Power companies nationwide employ tens of thousands of people who do nothing but read the meters. With smart meters, utility companies don't need meter readers anymore. As Sharan put it: "In five years, 20 million manually read meters are expected to disappear, taking with them some 28,000 meter-reading jobs. In other words, instead of creating jobs, smart metering will probably result in net job destruction."[25] Sharan calculated that installing 20 million new smart meters over five years would create about 1,600 new installation jobs. Unfortunately, most of the smart meters are made overseas. The meters will require people who know how to maintain and service them, but that would create a few hundred jobs at most.

Does that mean we should make a law protecting meter reader jobs forever? I don't agree with that. For the same reasons we no longer have elevator operators, bowling pin setters, and newspaper copy boys, we're unlikely to have meter readers in a few years' time. The point is, when you look closely at the technology and the goals of green energy, you're not likely to find the millions of jobs that our political leaders are promising.

WEIGHING REGULATIONS

The federal government's interest in promoting green jobs and green energy is tied inextricably to concerns about the environment and global climate change. The United States and governments around the world have responded with thousands of new rules and regulations meant to curb harmful emissions—not just carbon dioxide, but nitrogen, sulfur, and about 200 or so other hazardous chemicals. Regulations always carry costs, but they also come with certain benefits. How should the United States consider those tradeoffs in the midst of a sluggish recovery if the goal is to create 30 million new jobs?

Regardless whether you and I agree with the causes of climate change and man-made CO_2's impact on it, if you want to mandate limits on carbon emissions, then you'd better understand what happens when you limit what U.S. industries can do while China and Russia are developing all the oil, coal, and gas they can get their hands on.

Forcing manufacturers to use more and more renewable sources of energy might be fine over the long term. But wind and solar cost a lot more than oil, coal, and natural gas. All you're doing, in the short term at least, is hampering your own industrial sector. You're not really improving the world's environment. You're just letting them produce the same stuff over in China and Russia—where the environmental impact is potentially twice as bad.

Cap-and-trade is a good case in point. The idea behind cap-and-trade is that government sets a limit on how much carbon "pollution" your business can emit, and you buy permits to "pollute." If your business emits less carbon than you're permitted, you can sell or trade your extra carbon credits to other businesses. I say cap-and-trade is really a tax on doing business. It makes us less competitive and raises our costs. Now, it would be one thing if everyone around the world were subjected to cap-and-trade, if we could make sure that all the other folks aren't going to send their products to the United States to displace us because our cost structure is too high thanks to this carbon tax. China is going to be producing the same widgets we make, but less efficiently and with more CO_2 emissions than we would, because we've put this extra burden on ourselves.

In the name of fighting global warming, you're going to put us out of business and allow our foreign competitors to overrun our markets because we supposedly need to cut carbon emissions to where they were when the United States had about 230 million fewer people. But isn't the point of global warming that whether all of that nasty CO_2 goes into the atmosphere in New York or in Beijing, it's still going into the atmosphere? It's affecting the global climate, right? CO_2 doesn't stay local. We know China's pollution drifts across the Pacific Ocean to us. And China has no interest in global climate treaties. The Kyoto Protocol expired at the end of 2012 and China wasn't eager to put in place a new global agreement. They don't have any of the regulations we have in place now. That's why they have a major cost advantage due to the lack of environmental regulations and labor law regulations.

Simply having a policy here that ignores how the rest of the world works—for example, how China is spewing 10 or 20 times more CO_2 than we would making the same widget—is not environmentally responsible. If the idea is that we're supposed to lead by example, it isn't working, and it will never work. Somehow we're supposed to have more leverage to pressure the Chinese and other up-and-comers into adopting rules similar to ours. In reality, China uses coal-fired power plants to a far greater extent than we do. The Chinese have no pollution rules now, so not only will they be putting more CO_2 per ton of product produced into the environment, but they're also going to ignore all the other environmental issues that we deal with in the United States. Cap-and-trade would help China be profitable in that process. Why on earth would the Chinese give up that advantage? In the end, we'll end up importing more carbon-intensive goods because they're cheaper, hurting our industries, and all the while not reducing global carbon emissions. That's practically worse than doing nothing. If you really believe that greenhouse gases are causing the planet to warm up, and you think a carbon tax is the answer, then the answer is to put an equivalent tax on every product that enters the country to level the playing field.

I don't say all regulations are bad. Regulation is fine and even necessary. Government also regulates health and safety standards, which are extremely important in the steel industry. And government regulates banks and other financial services, though maybe not as much or as well as it should have given the market implosion in 2008. But taken to an extreme, regulations are unproductive. Government can't regulate everything. There are no guarantees in this life, and 100 percent safety and security will always remain a dream. Regulations are expensive. The more government regulates, the more businesses pay. The more businesses pay, the more costs are passed along to customers. And costly regulations have expanded under the last two administrations; the number of regulatory rules has exploded for companies making more than $100 million a year, from just 80 rules in 1995 to more than 150 today.

You can't say in one breath that you want to create millions of new jobs, revive the economy, and have a vibrant middle class, and then in the next say outlandish things about how businesses that make a profit aren't good for communities or workers. I see a major disconnect between President Obama's words to business leaders and the actions of the people who work for him. We've told him so, point blank. His answer? Most of the regulations that they're enforcing today were made in previous administrations. Fine. But he's the president *now*. Maybe instead of pointing the finger of blame at others, he could say, "I'm here, I'm in charge, and I'll deal with it." At this point, it doesn't really matter who dreamed up the rules five or ten years ago.

In fairness, the Obama administration did undertake an effort to streamline regulations and "create a 21st-century regulatory system."[26] The goal was to cut about 500 redundant rules and wasteful regulations across 26 federal agencies, saving U.S. taxpayers at least $10 billion. Among the rules the administration task force identified was one requiring ambulatory surgical centers to give patients verbal and written notices of their rights in advance of a procedure date, saving $50 million a year; streamlining the federal Office of Personnel Management's rules for hiring students and recent graduates, easing public-sector job creation; and simplifying Labor Department standards for hazardous chemical warnings, saving employers $2.5 billion over five years.

But those 500 older rules and regulations are about to be overwhelmed by 4,100 new ones, most of which the administration decided to hold back until after the 2012 election was over. The National Federation of Independent Business estimates the 13 most expensive of these regulations will cost the economy $515 billion.[27] Among businesses with fewer than 100 employees, the cost of compliance averages about $10,500 per worker, according to the Small Business Association.[28] Those costs are much higher for manufacturers. Representative Jim Jordan, a Republican congressman from Ohio, found that state and federal regulations cost manufacturers such as Nucor $688,944 a year on average. For smaller manufacturers, the cost of compliance is $26,316 per employee.[29]

The common Republican mantra is that regulations stunt job growth. I'm making a different argument. I realize that a big reason behind the layoffs of the past few years has been a lack of demand, not regulation alone. In other words, the causes are more complicated than they look. But I would add—and plenty of economists agree with me on this—that excessive regulation creates a drag on business that is genuinely tough to overcome, especially for smaller operations. Nucor can manage regulatory costs. We don't like it, but that's how it goes. But those compliance costs absolutely hammer smaller manufacturers. It's tough to keep expenses in check, hire new workers, and still make a profit with that kind of weight hanging over your head.

FIGURE 7.2   LACK OF DEMAND DRIVING LAYOFFS, NOT REGULATION

Surveys of business owners repeatedly show the driving force
behind the majority of layoffs is lack of demand, not regulations

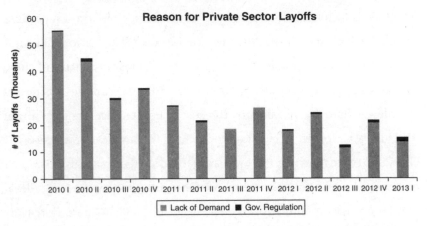

Source: *Bureau of Labor Statistics, Extended Mass Layoffs, May 13, 2013, http://www
.bls.gov/mls/.*

Why is it so hard to focus on the real issues? What's going on? I
don't know of anyone who would say unemployment is not a problem
in this country. Everybody understands it's really severe. They may argue about the degree. But we're stuck fighting over rules and regulations that make recovery and job creation needlessly difficult.

The EPA's recent power plant regulations, specifically the Utility
Maximum Achievable Control Technology (MACT) and Cross-State
Air Pollution rules, will kill jobs. Guaranteed. The American Coali-
tion for Clean Coal Electricity estimated losses of 1.4 million job-years[30]

through 2020.[31] Further, the EPA's proposed carbon dioxide emissions rules on new and existing power plants could cost upward of 224,000 jobs annually through 2030, according to the Institute for 21st Century Energy.[32] Now, am I saying let's go backward? Not at all. I remember what the air looked and smelled like in the 1970s. But let's recognize how far we've come, as well as the need to create a globally competitive platform for businesses to compete and for the United States to be an attractive place for people to invest.

We need a government that doesn't put up roadblocks to creating jobs but rather enhances our ability to grow. How about simply arriving at a point where getting the necessary permits to build a new factory or a power plant or a refinery doesn't take forever? You do permitting, you do a fair amount, but you don't put a process in place that basically says, "Yeah, sorry, it's going to be another five years before you can build anything." If government bureaucrats block the path to get from point A to point B, we're dead. And right now, that's what we have. That type of approach and attitude has got to go.

NUCOR'S EXPERIENCE IN LOUISIANA

The steel business has to contend with countless health, safety, and environmental regulations, and rightly so. Most Americans still associate the U.S. steel industry with spewing smokestacks fouling the landscape in western Pennsylvania 40 or 50 years ago. Pollution controls are much tighter than they once were, thanks in part to prudent government regulation, but also because the industry itself recognized that cleaner is better for business. Between 1990 and 2011, for example, the U.S. steel industry as a whole voluntarily reduced CO_2 emissions between 28 percent[33] and 30 percent.[34]

Nucor is as much a technology company as a steel manufacturer. New technologies reap greater efficiencies, which not only helps the bottom line but also benefits the environment. Our view is that sustainability is important, but you can't be sustainable if you're not profitable. Our view is also that as an American company, we want to help put Americans back to work. Regulate us, watch us, but don't have an attitude of "our goal is stop you, so we're going to regulate you into submission." Needless to say, that approach doesn't create jobs.

At Nucor, we're always looking for ways to expand our operations. About five years ago, we started scouting locations for a new facility to make high-quality direct reduced iron (DRI), which could revolutionize our business. In 2010, we settled on a location in St. James Parish, Louisiana, about an hour west of New Orleans along the Mississippi River.

One of Nucor's great innovations in the steel business was to use scrap metal to make steel. Well, scrap is a major world commodity now. Prices are about 400 percent higher today than they were in the late 1960s. Prices are a lot more volatile than they were even a decade ago. Frankly, the future is unknown when it comes to raw materials. So we began looking for alternatives. We found one in DRI, which basically reduces iron ore into pellets, typically using coal gas. Even using coal, the process is much cleaner than the traditional coke oven or blast furnace process. We've figured out how to make DRI more inexpensively, too, using natural gas that just happens to be booming in the United States right now.

The Louisiana project is moving ahead. We've put more than 600 construction contractors to work. The first of five phases will cost $750 million and will create 150 permanent jobs, making about 2.5 million tons of iron a year. When it's all done, we'll have invested $3.4 billion in the state, created 1,250 jobs, and generated more than $500 million in tax revenues for the state.

But it hasn't been easy. In fact, it has been ridiculously difficult. We hit so many roadblocks just trying to get the first phase of the project off the ground. It took three years to get all of our permits in order. You probably wonder what happened between day one and day 1,095. Nothing. Nothing substantial changed from the standpoint of actually getting the permits. It was all just delays, inefficiencies, lawsuits, more delays, more inefficiency, more lawsuits, and government bureaucracy getting in the way. The thinking seems to be, "What's the point of having a massive regulatory bureaucracy if it doesn't massively regulate?" The bureaucrats do their own thing at their own pace, then tell us to hurry up and comply with this or that redundant request for "more information." It's just a gross inefficiency, no different from what the post office lives with or Amtrak lives with, which is why the post office and Amtrak both lose money.

Mind you, Louisiana wanted us to come in and build. As states go, Louisiana is very business-friendly. The state understands the economic benefits that come with new construction and high-paying manufacturing jobs. We worked closely with Governor Bobby Jindal and Steve Moret, Jindal's secretary of economic development. State officials helped with site selection, permitting, financing, and infrastructure. But it still took three years to get permits for proven technology that is cleaner than just about all of the alternatives: technology, in fact, with a carbon footprint about one-third that of a traditional coke oven and blast furnace. We can use furnaces now that not only recapture and recycle heat but also filter out soot and other byproducts. We designed the plant to sit in the middle of 4,000 acres so that local residents won't even know it's there. This isn't your great-granddad's steel mill.

When we announced our decision to build in St. James Parish in September 2010, Jindal hailed it as one of the largest industrial projects in the state's history. It was a proud day for everyone. But instead of breaking ground right away, we had to battle a series of lawsuits from locals and questions from the EPA. Instead of telling us, "You've been issued a permit, you're good to go," we got sued. And all the while, state and federal elected officials were saying, "Yes, we want jobs!" It doesn't compute. It doesn't work.

We need to do everything to make that process as efficient and environmentally friendly and safe as possible. But it's too slow. We need to speed things up. You can't have a Nucor waiting three years to build a new DRI plant just because someone's in a position to throw frivolous crap at you. Our permitting process is archaic and needlessly politicized. Enough already. We need jobs. Everything else should take a backseat.

TOWARD AN AMERICAN INDUSTRIAL POLICY

I've laid out the scope of the problem. I've made the case for what has not worked and what isn't working. Now let's talk about solutions.

The president can take the lead here, but that's going to take discipline, and it means setting some priorities. He can see where the jobs have been lost and where the needs are greatest. And he can tell Congress and the American people that in order for us to get this economy going again, we have to find a way to put all these people who lost their jobs back to work.

In terms of regulation, that means we've got to streamline the whole process, because we want to be able to get these jobs going right away, not five years from now. So we've got to ease the permitting, ease regulatory burdens. President Obama, so fond of issuing executive orders, has got to say that this is more important because it's addressing the crisis at hand, that we're going to do it right but we're going to do it fast. We've got to update the way we finance and build infrastructure. We need to invest in high-value-added manufacturing. We have the ability; we've got the workforce; we've got the construction talent. We know how to do these things and we need to make sure that the states and the counties have the money to fulfill their obligations—and not just have the federal government dangling money that the states can't match.

But the one area that both sides agree on—in a country where nobody can seem to agree on anything—is that a new energy paradigm is emerging. It isn't only wind and solar. It's shale and natural gas. Energy is a huge need. Look at our trade deficit, which, again, was about $475 billion in 2013—a near record high.[35] Energy accounts for about half of it. Energy is a great job creator. North Dakota, Ohio, and Pennsylvania are booming right now. The United States is on track to replace Saudi Arabia as the largest oil producer on the planet.[36]

But what a lot of people don't know is that even as we're tapping into this resource, shale and gas, we're actually reducing our carbon footprint. Not perfectly. The guys who want it done perfectly can go away. We're not going to be perfect, and we're not going to get carbon out of our economy any time soon, if ever. But we're going to reduce our carbon footprint by switching from coal to natural gas, and by incorporating it into transit. For example, Nucor opted for a natural gas–fed DRI plant in Louisiana, which will produce iron units with 60 percent less CO_2 generation per iron unit than a traditional coal-based blast furnace and coke-making facility.[37] That's pretty damn good. Remember, we're trying to get out of a crisis; we're not trying to use this crisis as an opportunity to reinvent ourselves. Once we get healthy again, then we may have that luxury.

In the end, any solution will require the United States to adopt an honest-to-goodness industrial policy. I know that the idea of industrial policy is kind of a no-no for a lot of people, especially free-market economists. I really don't think we need to be just like Japan and create our own version of the Ministry of Economy, Trade and Industry. I don't want to copy Japan—or China or the European Union, for that matter. An American industrial policy is one that says industry and job creation through innovation and making and building things is a vital part of our economic strategy. We're going to do things that allow us to have a competitive global footprint and a strong manufacturing and industrial base that can compete globally.

So what does that look like? Often it simply means avoiding policies that put our manufacturers at a disadvantage. In other words, if you're keen to impose environmental regulations on the U.S. manufacturing base because you believe it's the right thing to do, then don't allow foreign imports unless they adopt the same rules.

Historically, trade has been a major component of a good industrial policy. In effect, all that would mean for an American industrial policy is rule-based free trade with active enforcement—our government keeping other governments honest and not letting them take unfair advantage of our industries. Now, that doesn't mean that a government can't support its economy. But it does mean I can't go out and manipulate my currency to give my state-owned enterprises an unfair advantage against your guys so that when you wake up tomorrow morning and go open your storefront, you're already $50 in the hole.

An industrial policy should be much broader than trade, though. And it should be broader than just taxes and regulations. It's about the public and private sector sharing a common goal. In the remaining chapters, I'll show how the United States can get there from here.

EIGHT

WHERE WE GO FROM HERE

Rebuilding the Backbone of the U.S. Economy

ANYONE WHO DRIVES TO WORK EVERYDAY KNOWS the United States has a need for wider, smoother highways. Train commuters understand that most municipal light rail and subway systems are aging and in need of an upgrade. Frequent flyers know all about delays. International business travelers have likely experienced how truly high-speed Internet works—it's vastly superior to the Wi-Fi most Americans use. Superstorm Sandy, which pummeled New York and New Jersey in 2012, exposed exactly how frail the physical infrastructure of the nation's largest metropolitan region is. In certain parts of the country, rolling blackouts and brownouts have become routine during the hot summer months.

When asked, an overwhelming majority of Americans—more than seven in ten, in at least one poll—think state and federal governments should spend more on transportation and infrastructure upgrades.[1] But most Americans don't need to be asked. They *know* the United States has an infrastructure problem. They've lived with it for years. The country's need for new and greatly improved infrastructure is enormous. Any fixes will take time and cost money—somewhere between $3 trillion and $3.8 trillion over the next five to ten years, although that's a conservative estimate. Infrastructure spending is one area where bipartisan agreement should be easy to achieve.

I wouldn't even classify infrastructure spending as "spending." It's a public investment that pays dividends for decades. I know that *investment* is one of those weasel words politicians often use to downplay spending, so I can see why people would be wary of it. Nine times out of ten, I groan too when they talk about "investment," when you know that what they want to do is throw more money at a problem without really solving it. But infrastructure really is different. It's one of the safest possible investments—like a mutual fund with a 10 or 15 percent rate of return. Who wouldn't put their money into that?

We need the infrastructure spending to create jobs and attract more investment at home and abroad. If you don't have world-class highways or ports or broadband, you can't compete with the other parts of the world. Believe me, China knows this. India knows. Brazil and Malaysia and Indonesia know. Americans know too.

FIGURE 8.1   INFRASTRUCTURE SPENDING PRODUCES STRONG RETURNS

Spending on infrastructure has immediate and positive benefits to the overall economy

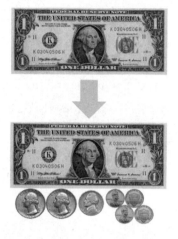

Every $1 dollar in infrastructure investments leads to . . .

$1.59 in gains in GDP

Source: *Mark Zandi, "Assessing the Macro Economic Impact of Fiscal Stimulus 2008," Moody's Economy.com, January 2008, https://www.economy.com/mark-zandi /documents/Stimulus-Impact-2008.pdf.*

America's founding generation believed "internal improvements"[2] would mean economic expansion, and the young United States spent millions of federal tax dollars building bridges, waterways, and the first national highway—the Cumberland Road—that originally linked the Potomac River to the Ohio River and later extended through Ohio and Indiana into Illinois. Congress saw the road as a way to "civilize the interior"[3] of the country—which meant bringing social, political, and economic development to the wilderness. Such projects were not always easy, they certainly were not perfect, and public works spending could be controversial at times. But the consensus remains that the country was better off for all of it.

The generation that came of age during the Great Depression and World War II understood this too. Think of the majestic public works projects of the New Deal era: The Hoover Dam helped bring water and power to Las Vegas and much of Southern California. Bigger still was the Triborough Bridge, connecting Manhattan to Queens and the Bronx by way of the Harlem River, Bronx Kill, and Hell Gate along the East River. The Golden Gate Bridge and the San Francisco Bay Bridge were both New Deal projects, and all were American made. Even the more modest projects the Works Progress Administration accomplished during the worst years of the Great Depression are worth celebrating: 78,000 new bridges and viaducts, and improvements on 46,000 more; 572,000 miles of rural roads and 67,000 miles of city streets; 39,000 new and remodeled schools; 2,500 hospitals; 12,800 playgrounds.[4]

Dwight Eisenhower and a bipartisan Congress in the 1950s decided the national economy would reap huge benefits from the Interstate Highway System. It took 35 years to complete and cost more than $114 billion, but economists agree that the overall investment was a boon to both the American economy and to society.[5] The best economic research we have suggests that every dollar Americans invested in the highway system nearly 60 years ago has been paid back sixfold.[6]

But we're still living with the infrastructure of the 1930s and '40s and '50s. Time has taken its toll. We've added another 150 million people to our population since 1950, a few years before the Interstate Highway System really took shape. We don't simply need to rebuild—we need more capacity. We've got to invest and reinvest. From a business perspective, I can tell you Nucor is constantly exploring new technology and refining its processes to stay ahead of our competitors. You may have the greatest mousetrap in the world, but if you don't keep reinvesting and updating and maintaining your advantage, you become less competitive.

What's true of companies is also true of countries, especially in a globalized economy where nations compete with each other and regions

FIGURE 8.2 FALLING STATUS IN GLOBAL COMPETITIVENESS

- The United States has fallen from ranking 1st on the World Economic Forum's Global Competitiveness Index in 2008 to 7th place in 2012

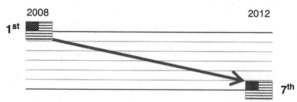

- The United States also does far worse when looking at just infrastructure, falling from 9th place in 2008 to 25th in 2012

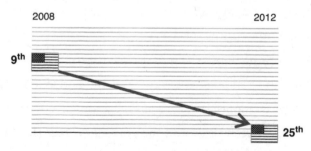

Source: *World Economic Forum, "Global Competitiveness Report 2008–2009," Switzerland, 2008, http://www.weforum.org/pdf/GCR08/GCR08.pdf; World Economic Forum, "Global Competitiveness Report 2012–2013," Switzerland, 2012, http://www3. weforum.org/docs/WEF_GlobalCompetitivenessReport_2012-13.pdf.*

vie for domination. The World Economic Forum's Global Competitiveness Index in 2008 ranked U.S. infrastructure sixth in the world.[7] In 2012, the United States fell to twenty-fifth place, behind Singapore, South Korea, Canada, and nearly every major European country except Great Britain and the Czech Republic.[8] Why did the United States fall so far, so fast, on that international ranking?

We've failed to make the necessary investments in repairing and upgrading our infrastructure. Today, the United States spends a paltry 1.7 percent of our national wealth on infrastructure.[9] Our Canadian neighbors spend a full 4 percent.[10] India spends 5 percent.[11] And China? Try 9 percent.[12] Remember, China's answer to the global economic crisis of 2008 was to pour $750 billion into roads, dams, and bridges alone, whether the country needed them or not.[13] We spent just $30 billion from a stimulus package of about $800 billion.

I know that Americans are worried about the national debt. I know they worry about government waste. But infrastructure is not waste. If we think of infrastructure in the context of competing globally, the supposed costs are quickly overshadowed by the benefits. The investment is going to pay off not just five or ten years from now, but 30 or 40 years from now as well.

If you think about the way private enterprise works, most companies have an operating budget and a capital budget. They make distinctions between money that goes out the door and comes in the door, and of course, between those and the year-end things that are longer-term investments.

The federal government doesn't work that way. A dollar that goes into the salary of a bureaucrat someplace is the same as a dollar that goes into building a road. But if government could break those things out and treat them differently, it would have a big effect on how we finance public works.

So if infrastructure is like putting your money in a bank account with a 4 percent return, spending on more bureaucracy would be like putting your money in the kind of conventional savings accounts most banks are offering nowadays, with piddling interest rates (or, frankly, negative interest rates). Bureaucracy has very little payback in the long run. You aren't getting much bang for your buck. But you're getting a lot out of a road or a bridge because of how much the road and the bridge contribute to economic growth over the decades.

Even a "bridge to nowhere" can one day become a "bridge to somewhere." A lot of people joked about the proposed bridge to Gravina Island in Alaska. It became a presidential campaign issue in 2008, when Alaska governor Sarah Palin was named John McCain's running mate on the Republican presidential ticket. Palin first supported funding for the $398 million bridge and then changed her mind.[14] The bridge—which would have been longer than the Golden Gate and taller than the Brooklyn Bridge—was part of a plan to develop the island, which is home to the Ketchikan Airport and about 50 people and is only serviced by ferry.

Maybe nothing much is on that island today. But if the bridge had been built, eventually, what happens? Somebody is going to build a gas station and a convenience store. Maybe the airport will build up its traffic, and businesses will start to service more planes and passengers. Pretty soon, it's not a bridge to nowhere anymore. Just look at what has happened around every city that built a bypass loop. There was nothing there when the roads were built. Today, the development is everywhere along them, and now they are being widened.

WHERE THE NEEDS ARE

The claim, then, is that the United States needs to spend between $3 trillion and $4 trillion on infrastructure. Those trillions would repair existing infrastructure, some of which is a half-century old or older, as well as buy additional infrastructure capacity to stay competitive internationally. The needs for a growing country of 314 million people are vast. The infrastructure we build now would need to accommodate a population estimated to reach 350 million by 2030 and 400 million by 2050, according the 2012 National Census Population Projections.[15] We need the infrastructure. We need the jobs. We can have both.

What kind of needs? How many jobs? Figures from the nonpartisan Milken Institute suggest the following:

- Repairing, updating, and expanding U.S. highways, tunnels, and bridges could create 6.2 million direct and indirect jobs. Initial investment: $225 billion.
- Rewiring 80 percent of the nation's neighborhoods, expanding high-speed fiber-optic lines, and building next-generation mobile networks and wireless Internet service in underserved parts of the country could create 1 million direct and indirect jobs. Initial investment: $55 billion.
- Rebuilding America's urban wastewater systems, water infrastructure, and pipelines, along with schools and public

FIGURE 8.3   JOB CREATION FROM INFRASTRUCTURE INVESTMENT

With $415 billion in initial investment, infrastructure
improvements alone can create more than 10 million jobs

IMPACTS OF INFRASTRUCTURE UPGRADES	Initial Investment ($ Billion)	Direct Jobs	Indirect Jobs	Total Jobs
Highways, Tunnels, Bridges	$225	2,480	3,720	6,200
High-Speed Fiber	$55	400	600	1,000
Waterways/Public Building	$33	330	495	825
All-of-the-Above Energy Strategy	$102	800	1,200	2,000
TOTAL	$415	4,010	6,015	10,025

Source: *Ross DeVol and Perry Wong, "Jobs for America: Investment and Policies for Economic Growth and Competitiveness," Milken Institute, January 2010, http:// assets1c.milkeninstitute.org/assets/Publication/ResearchReport/PDF/JFAFullReport .pdf.*

buildings, could create as many as 825,000 direct and indirect jobs for construction workers and related support industries. Initial investment: $33 billion.

- Adopting an "all-of-the-above" energy policy that includes coal, natural gas, oil, nuclear, wind, and solar could create 2 million direct and indirect jobs as we build new smart grids, run transmission lines, and construct power plants and distribution facilities. Initial investment: $102 billion.[16]

In total, a revitalized infrastructure agenda can create nearly 10 million jobs for Americans who sorely need them.

And beyond the jobs, what sort of benefits would that investment provide? Figures from the American Society of Civil Engineers and the FAA suggest the following:

- Better roads will cut the estimated $78 billion drag on the U.S. economy that results from commuters wasting 4.2 billion hours a year idling in traffic. We'll save as much as $67 billion on car repairs and maintenance alone.[17]
- Improved waterworks and sewage systems will spare businesses $147 billion and homeowners some $59 billion in repairs over a decade. We'll save as much as 7 billion gallons of water a day from being wasted due to rusty and leaky pipes.[18]
- Better light rail and mass transit will save about $71 million in gasoline a year.[19]
- A satellite-based air-traffic control system—dubbed "NextGen" by the FAA—would slash delays and allow for more direct flights, saving airlines and consumers an estimated $24 billion through 2020, 1.4 billion gallons in jet fuel, and 14 billion fewer tons of CO_2.[20]
- A smarter power grid will improve distribution, cutting outages and rolling blackouts and saving anywhere from $25 billion to $180 billion a year.[21]

The current conversation about twenty-first-century infrastructure often includes high-speed rail as well. China, Japan, Singapore, Germany, France, and Spain have extensive high-speed rail systems that many Americans would love to emulate in the United States. I'm skeptical. Sure, having a train that could run from New York to Boston or from L.A. to San Francisco in less than two hours would be great. Right now, the Acela line from New York to Boston, which Amtrak considers "high-speed," takes three and a half hours with speeds rarely exceeding 150 miles per hour. The question is, Where should high-speed rail fall on a lengthy and expensive list of priorities?

In California, Governor Jerry Brown committed to spending nearly $70 billion on a high-speed train from Los Angeles to San Francisco.[22] The first phase of construction is starting in the middle of the state. There are a couple of problems with California's plan, though. First, the state transportation department is sitting on a list of nearly $200 billion or so worth of traditional infrastructure projects, from retrofitting bridges and improving goods movement from the state's ports in Los Angeles, Long Beach, and Oakland, to shoring up crumbling levies in the San Joaquin Delta.[23] Second, the state is still deeply in debt and really doesn't have the financing for the train. Third, the only way the state's business plan for the train makes any sense is if the price of gasoline hits $40 a gallon. But the bottom line here is, would the public be better served spending $70 billion building a high-speed rail line or retrofitting structurally deficient dams, levies, and bridges?

We've got to get our basic infrastructure back into sound shape using modern technologies to make it more efficient, to build it, and to operate it—as opposed to spending tens or even hundreds of billions on radical forms of transportation that may promise more than they can really deliver right now.

GETTING UP TO SPEED

Though I'm not a fan of high-speed rail, high-speed process planning, financing, and building critical infrastructure is crucial.

I remember President Obama got into some trouble when he joked at a meeting of the White House jobs council that "shovel-ready was not as shovel-ready as we expected."[24] He was talking about all of the infrastructure projects that states had sitting on the shelf, ready to go in every respect except for funding.

Turns out, the Department of Transportation's process for doling out stimulus dollars wasn't much faster than business-as-usual. Most of the projects funded under the Recovery Act didn't get underway for at least a year or two after Congress passed the law.

Fact: most nonstimulus infrastructure maintenance and repair projects require years, and new construction often takes a decade or more without federal funding. When federal funds are introduced, the average time to complete a federally funded highway project is *13 years*.

If we're going to restore America's highways, roads, bridges, and airports to world-class status and create well-paying jobs—as opposed to more bureaucracy—we can't get bogged down in years of planning, studies, and red tape. Federal and state authorities should allow maximum flexibility, clear away redundant permitting, and get these projects moving.

Government often has acted quickly in the face of emergency. In 1994, Northridge, California was hit with a 6.7 earthquake that destroyed several freeway bridges and overpasses. The most critical damage was on Los Angeles's Interstate 10 freeway, which links downtown Los Angeles to the Pacific Ocean. It's one of the heaviest-traveled freeways in the world. Experts at California's state department of transportation told Pete Wilson, California's governor at the time, that rebuilding I-10 would require at least two and a half years to complete, taking into account all of the necessary surveys, public hearings, environmental impact studies, contract bidding, absurd bureaucratic hurdles, and red tape that always seem to get in the way of useful work.

Ultimately, the job was done in less than two and a half months. How did that happen? Here's where the partnership between the public and private sectors comes into play. The point of any partnership is to work toward a common goal and create a situation where government and business can help rather than undermine each other.

In California, Wilson declared a state of emergency, waived a raft of state environmental rules and labor laws, and offered lucrative incentives to construction companies to finish the project ahead of schedule. Wilson promised an extra $200,000 a day for every day that work was finished ahead of schedule. The contractor, C. C. Myers, had crews working 24 hours a day, seven days a week, and finished 74 days before the deadline to collect a cool $14.5 million bonus. Even after paying all that overtime and renting extra equipment, Myers made a profit of $8 million.

Taxpayers profited, too. They came out way ahead in the end because the eight-figure bonus to Myers was more than offset by the economic benefits of a wide-open road. A study by the governor's office at the time found that the freeway shutdown had cost Los Angeles and surrounding cities about $1 million a day in lost tax revenue and productivity.

More recently, in 2012, Jerry Brown cited Wilson's actions to speed along the reconstruction of another major overpass that had been destroyed by a fuel tanker fire. A new, wider bridge reopened about five months later, three weeks ahead of schedule and at a cost of $7 million. What happened in California is a great example of public-private partnerships in action. Sure, a private company made some money, but taxpayers came out ahead, too.

Now, I'm not saying the president should declare a state of emergency, waive the Clean Air and Clean Water Acts, and throw out 80 years of labor laws with a stroke of a pen. I don't think he would even if he could—can you imagine the outcry from unions and environmental groups? But I am saying infrastructure is, relatively speaking, one of the easiest things we can do to get the economy back on track. We know incentives work. And in the face of a crisis, we have the means of not just cutting red tape, but incinerating it in some cases at the state and federal level.

President Obama, in fact, has used his authority to expedite more than a dozen high-profile projects, including the replacement of New York's Tappan Zee Bridge, the expansion of Baltimore's Red Line, and the Qwuloolt Estuary Restoration Project in Washington. Clearly, the president has taken some steps in the right direction. I wish we would stop regulating ourselves out of making the bigger effort. Don't drag these projects out for five or ten years' worth of permitting and lawsuits and all of the other crap that has steadily undermined America's competitive advantages. Streamline the permitting process, recognize that nothing's going to be perfect, and do the job to the best of our ability—but *do it*.

WHO PAYS AND HOW?

That's the $3 trillion question. All too often, discussions about infrastructure funding degenerate into disputes among different regions and political parties. Usually, the winners are the ones with the congressmen sitting on the more influential subcommittees. It shouldn't be that way.

One of the most frequently asked questions that comes up in these arguments is some variation of: *Why should the good people of Davenport, Iowa be forced to send their tax dollars across the country to pay for retrofitting a bridge or repaving a road in Los Angeles?*

Fair question. Here's a better one: why should the good people of Los Angeles be forced to foot the bill to retrofit a bridge or repave a road when a good portion of the traffic is made up of trucks or trains carrying goods from Southern California's bustling ports to places like Salt Lake City, or Denver, or Davenport, Iowa? The point is, infrastructure is a national issue, with costs and benefits that extend beyond a particular city's limits or a state's borders. Paying for these projects requires a national solution.

Traditionally, states and local governments pay for infrastructure through sales and gasoline taxes. Most public funding for roads, sewers, and transit comes from the states. Increasing local infrastructure investments through tolls, tax-increment financing, and expanded public-private partnerships could create as many as 3.5 million jobs at a cost of $150 billion.[25]

At the federal level, the Highway Trust Fund has been the primary source of building, maintaining, and upgrading roads and bridges. The

FIGURE 8.4   STATE VS. FEDERAL INFRASTRUCTURE SPENDING

Infrastructure spending has steadily declined over the last several decades, with states and local governments bearing the majority of costs

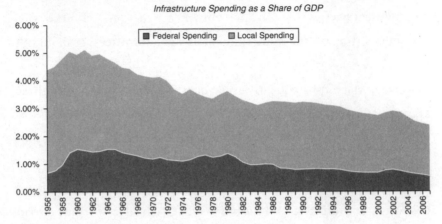

Infrastructure Spending as a Share of GDP

Source: *Congressional Budget Office, "Public Spending on Transportation and Water Infrastructure," November 17, 2010, http://www.cbo.gov/sites/default/files/cbofiles /attachments/11-17-10-Infrastructure.pdf.*

trouble is, the Highway Trust Fund, like so many other federal funds, is unsustainable. In fact, the fund is likely to be depleted this year. There simply aren't enough gasoline tax revenues. The last time the federal gas tax was raised was 1993. It's now 18.4 cents a gallon. Had Congress indexed the tax to inflation, the tax would be 29 cents a gallon today and would generate another $12 billion annually. At the same time, thanks to federal mandates and advances in hybrid vehicle technology, cars are a lot more fuel-efficient today, so the government is collecting less revenue. In our perfectly legitimate effort to be cleaner and greener, we've undermined the federal government's ability to maintain one of the greatest infrastructure achievements in our history. The trouble with gas taxes is they hit the poor hardest. Low-income folks aren't the ones buying all those Priuses.

A gas tax isn't the only way to raise money for roads. We have several alternatives. Tolls provide highway funding based on a pay-per-use system. E-Z Pass systems eliminate the need for tollbooths, saving labor costs and making payments quick and convenient. I'm not necessarily in favor of privately owned toll roads, but if that's what it takes to get the infrastructure improvements we need, so be it.

Several U.S. cities are looking at "congestion pricing," which is comparable to a toll on driving during peak traffic hours. Because freeway capacity is necessarily limited, the idea is to reduce traffic jams—along with pollution from all of those idling vehicles—by encouraging drivers to adjust when and where they drive. London, Stockholm, Singapore, Milan, and, here in the United States, Atlanta all use some form of congestion pricing on commuters.

The Transportation Infrastructure Finance and Innovation Act of 1998 offers federal credit assistance to states for transit and other infrastructure improvements. The Federal Transit Administration says TIFIA has provided $7.9 billion in credit assistance for 22 projects since 1999, representing $29.4 billion in infrastructure investment.[26] Why not expand that program to use federal leverage to get more out of private capital?

Combined with an inflation-adjusted gas tax, these policies could pump up the Highway Trust Fund with another $50 billion for vital roadwork and create as many as 1.2 million jobs just from spending and efficiency gains.[27] We could try some of the above, all of the above, or none of the above. But if it's none of above, then we need to find some other way to attract the resources and investment the country needs to build.

TAKE THAT TO THE (INFRASTRUCTURE) BANK

Another way to address financing a long-term, multi-trillion dollar effort would be to put together an infrastructure bank along the lines of the European Investment Bank, which controls more than $300 billion in assets and put nearly $100 billion into transportation and other projects in 2011 alone.[28] The goal of a U.S. infrastructure bank would be to leverage nearly $2 trillion in capital over ten years, with

FIGURE 8.5   BENEFITS OF A NATIONAL INFRASTRUCTURE BANK

A national infrastructure bank more effectively and efficiently uses public funds for infrastructure by:

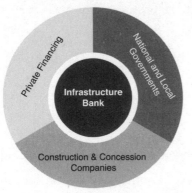

○ Creating a coordinated national infrastructure strategy across multiple agencies

○ Removing infrastructure decisions from political earmarks and choosing projects based on needs and merits

○ Providing stability of project funding, reducing risks for third-party investors

initial seed money of $30 billion. An infrastructure bank would fund projects at up to 50 percent of costs, with a priority on projects that are most likely to lower transportation and production costs over the long term.

We're looking for the most bang for our buck here. Easier said than done, you say. Who's going to provide the money to the infrastructure bank? The federal government doesn't have it. Wouldn't the feds just borrow more? Not necessarily. We should try to bring in the private sector whenever and wherever we can. The whole appeal of infrastructure projects is that they tend to be safe investments with solid returns. If we can streamline the permitting processes, making them more efficient than they are today, the private sector can make a profit and the public can enjoy the benefits sooner. Everybody wins.

Public utilities already offer a good model for how private companies can bring greater efficiency to the public sector while still allowing for a good profit. These private companies are regulated heavily because water and power are basic necessities. But for the most part, they do a good job. They aren't always perfect, but they're a lot more cost-effective than many municipal utilities.

Let's expand that model. I'm convinced the private sector would have a great interest in putting money into an independently governed U.S. infrastructure bank. Pension funds and hedge funds would love an infrastructure bank. A case in point would be the California Public Employee Retirement System (CalPERS), one of the largest institutional investments in the United States, with more than $245 billion in assets.[29] Right now, the pension fund has about $1 billion invested in infrastructure around the world.[30] In October 2012, CalPERS announced plans to expand those investments even more—upward of $5 billion.[31] Where better to put that money than in the United States?

Thinking more broadly, we could leverage some of our relationships around the world with sovereign wealth funds that are more interested in putting their capital to work in a stable market. Foreigners who've bought U.S. government securities in the past would likely be willing to fund an infrastructure bank. How do I know? Because in addition to Europe's bank, the private sector has already invested in California's infrastructure and economic development bank, which the state set up back in 1994. The I-Bank, as it's called, has issued more than $30 billion in tax-exempt bonds to help finance the state's considerable infrastructure needs.

So the idea for a national infrastructure bank isn't new. Unfortunately, several bipartisan efforts by Congress to establish a bank have been scuttled by petty politics. That's a shame, since it's one of those rare ideas that has the support of both the U.S. Chamber of Commerce and the AFL-CIO. Senators Chuck Hagel and Chris Dodd first introduced a bill to establish a national infrastructure bank in 2007 that languished in committee. Barack Obama campaigned on the idea in 2008. Senators John Kerry and Kay Bailey Hutchison sponsored their own version of an infrastructure bank in 2011 called the Building and Upgrading Infrastructure for Long-Term Development (BUILD) Act.

Remember that meeting in Washington I mentioned that was supposed to be about infrastructure? Senator Kerry was there to explain how he had several foreign countries lined up to put their money into a national I-Bank, but his bill ran into a brick wall of partisan opposition.

Never mind that he had support from Hutchison and several other Republicans in the House and Senate.

Now, I'm willing to bet that if infrastructure and job creation had been treated as a serious priority in the first year of Obama's presidency, when the Democrats held the House and the Senate, we would have an infrastructure bank today. We don't. Instead, we have businesses trying to figure out how to absorb the costs of the Affordable Care Act and other new regulations.

Infrastructure done right could provide 10 million of 30 million new jobs within a decade.[32] Expanding our nation's energy resources could provide millions more. In the next chapter, I'll show you how.

NINE

WHERE WE GO NEXT

Tapping Our Energy Resources

IN A COUNTRY WHERE SOMETIMES IT SEEMS LIKE nobody can agree on anything, the one thing just about everyone can agree about is the arrival of a new energy paradigm. That paradigm may be summed up in one word: shale.

Within all of that sedimentary rock hundreds of feet below the earth's surface sits trillions of cubic feet of natural gas, and billions of barrels of oil, just waiting to be tapped. And it's all American. The International Energy Agency at the end of 2012 forecasted that the United States would topple Saudi Arabia as the world's largest oil producer by 2020.[1] Not only does that have implications for the world oil market, but it also translates to between 1.1 and 1.4 million new American jobs by the end of the decade and more than $127 billion in new tax revenues.[2]

Natural gas is a game-changing resource for the American economy. It is literally fueling the beginnings of a manufacturing renaissance in the United States. Not everyone agrees that the new shale paradigm is necessarily a good thing, especially environmental groups. But it would be a mistake for political and business leaders to put too many barriers in the way of responsibly developing such a vital resource, especially when it holds the key to millions of jobs.

And while the natural gas industry has taken off in the past five years, we're also in the early stages of an oil boom. Remember that slogan a couple of presidential elections ago, "Drill, baby, drill"? I do. I

FIGURE 9.1   NATURAL GAS PRODUCTION GROWTH

Natural gas production is expected to increase by 44%, driven primarily from new shale resources

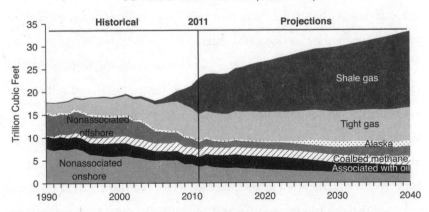

Source: *Energy Information Agency, "Annual Energy Outlook 2013," December 5, 2012, http://www.eia.gov/forecasts/aeo/er/pdf/0383er(2013).pdf.*

FIGURE 9.2   US TO BECOME A MAJOR OIL PRODUCER

By 2020, the United States is expected to become a net oil producer, with US production growing 25% compared to world growth at just 20%

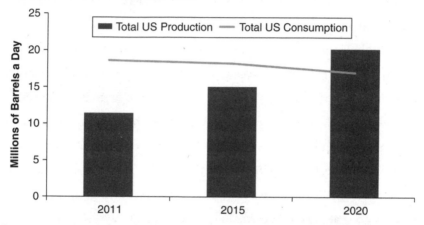

US Oil Production and Consumption

Source: *Citigroup, "Energy 2020: North America, the New Middle East?," March 20, 2012, https://www.citivelocity.com/citigps/ReportSeries.action?recordId=6.*

also remember a lot of pundits and political leaders saying it couldn't be done, shouldn't be done, or wouldn't make a difference anyway. Well, never say never.

The new American gas and oil boom reminds us all that energy is the cornerstone of all economic development. Everyone depends on it. In terms of cost and availability, natural gas has never been cheaper or more readily available domestically than it is right now. With each passing year, we find more of the stuff. Energy companies are getting better at using technology to extract oil and gas from the vast shale formations under much of the central and eastern United States. Horizontal drilling and new wells leave a much smaller footprint on the landscape than traditional methods.

When energy costs are low, not only do you stimulate economic growth, you also stimulate the innovation you need to create high-paying jobs and strengthen the middle class. Nucor is a living example. Our growth into the largest U.S. steel maker hinged largely on the availability of low-cost energy. When we first got into the steel business in the 1960s, our electric-arc furnaces gave us a big advantage over our larger competitors because they were more efficient than giant blast furnaces, and electricity was cheap and plentiful. So was the scrap metal we recycled into high-quality steel. Our material and energy advantage allowed us to leverage technology that revolutionized steelmaking in America.

A half-century later, we use one-quarter the energy to produce a ton of steel that the older technology required and leave one-quarter the environmental footprint we once did. We're getting better all the time, even as electric-arc furnace steelmaking is growing into 60 percent of the steel business in the United States.

The natural gas boom is allowing Nucor to expand further. Our direct reduced iron plant in Louisiana was made possible by inexpensive natural gas. One day, that facility will produce 3 million tons of DRI, and eventually steel.

Just think about all the benefits of natural gas: jobs, infrastructure, energy efficiency, innovation, you name it. Not just for Nucor, but for manufacturing across the board. Now, the process isn't perfect. We're not using zero energy to make a ton of iron or steel. And it's called *carbon steel* for a reason. But recognize the positives: we're vastly more efficient today than we ever were. The availability of cheaper energy, even—or especially—from hydrocarbons, will actually let us refine our processes even further.

That's why I call it a game changer, because it has the potential to completely change the economic cost dynamics of just about anything we do in this country, whether it's making steel, making fertilizer, or making yo-yos. Natural gas may change the way we transport goods overseas and around the country since natural gas is cleaner than diesel fuel. Already, American consumers are saving about $100 billion a year on their heating and electric bills thanks to falling natural gas prices. So the potential for changing the course of our economy is huge.

If you can have a readily abundant energy supply that is roughly one-tenth the cost of traditional power sources, how competitive does that make you in a cutthroat global environment? Massively! We have an energy edge over our foreign competitors that we should take full advantage of.

But there are dangerous signs that the United States will throw its new energy advantage away by exporting cheap natural gas to America's competitors. The big fight in Washington right now is over whether U.S. energy firms should be permitted to export liquefied natural gas (LNG). I think I've made myself clear that boosting U.S. exports would be a very good thing, but I'm dead set against exporting LNG, at least until we have used that gas here at home to improve our economic competitiveness. I'll remain opposed until Americans have fully enjoyed the benefits of all of that low-cost energy. We need that gas here to solve a jobs crisis, a manufacturing crisis, and an economic crisis.

The federal government doesn't see it that way. The Obama administration in late 2012 put out a report saying, in effect, that shipping cheap and plentiful natural gas overseas has no downside, and may actually boost the energy sector and the economy.[3]

I disagree. For one thing, that Obama administration report downplayed the fact that shipping gas abroad would raise prices at home just as certain industries that had all but disappeared from U.S. soil are reinvesting heavily again. Sorry, but the benefits of natural gas fueling heavy industry, chemicals, steel, and other manufacturers far outweigh any gain in exports. An economic study by Charles River Associates confirms this, finding that increased manufacturing generated by inexpensive U.S. natural gas creates twice the direct value for our economy and eight times as many jobs as LNG exports.[4]

I think the siren song of unfettered free trade tends to cloud the minds of otherwise intelligent people. James Taranto at the *Wall Street Journal* wrote in response to a critic of the study: "By this logic, U.S. companies shouldn't be allowed to export anything, lest prices go up and domestic buyers be forced to pay more."[5] No. Wrong. That is exactly backward.

U.S. natural gas prices aren't linked to the global price of oil. If we're paying $2.50 or even $3.50 per thousand cubic feet (TCF) for natural gas domestically and it's $16 or $17 TCF overseas, that neuters the foreign labor cost advantage that has been driving U.S. companies to offshore their production and R&D. When energy costs are that low, all of a sudden we can start competing with subsidized industries employing two-dollar-a-day factory workers. We can't do that when our labor costs and our energy costs are sky high. If we start exporting natural gas, before long we'll go from $2.50 TCF to $10 TCF, our competitors will go from $16 TCF to $10 TCF, and we're back to being uncompetitive again.

In today's world, you've got to be smarter than the next guy, and you cannot put policies in place that needlessly and stupidly add to your costs of doing business. The better way—the more realistic way—is to set policies that foster economic growth and development, using every advantage we've got.

I see another big danger in the zeal to eliminate carbon emissions altogether, essentially regulating major American manufacturers out of existence. That would be a huge bungle. There won't be another Nucor to come along in a hyperregulated environment. All those benefits I keep talking about—the jobs, infrastructure, efficiency, innovation? Gone for good. The fact is, jobs that replace manufacturing—in the tech sector, for example—simply won't fill the gap. (Assuming, of course, the tech industry remains free of regulation.)

We have a crying need for jobs. We have a massive trade imbalance on energy. And we've got this great new energy resource in shale and natural gas. Wise policy would leverage this game-changing resource at home to unravel that energy trade deficit that I talked about in chapter 4.

Think about it this way: What causes a recession to come about in its very basic form? You're missing something in the economy that's normally there. What is it? It's demand. When you've got an excess of supply and little demand, economic growth drops off, workers get let go, people stop investing, and pricing goes down the toilet. So bucking any recession requires demand growth, and whatever it takes to create that demand growth.

Now suppose I told you today that we have $600 billion worth of demand sitting right in front of us for the taking. You don't have to create it. It's already there. All you've got to do is focus your attention on tapping the demand that's there. Where is it? Where is the demand? It's in the trade deficit, of course. Our trade deficit is roughly half goods, half energy. We're buying all kinds of crap from overseas, and we're not exporting enough. So we have tremendous demand in this economy. The problem is, it's disproportionately met with stuff produced and made elsewhere, creating jobs and multiplier effects abroad that would otherwise be created here.

We could cut the trade deficit in half if we meet this demand with American-made products. The question should not be what to do to stimulate demand, but rather, what do we have to do to recapture the demand that we've created? It's a big difference.

We've got the demand for energy. We've just been letting other people meet it.

For 40 years, American political leaders have been saying the United States should be energy independent. And for 40 years, we've made very little progress toward that goal. The truth is, we don't need to wean ourselves from 100 percent of our imported energy. It's fine to import oil from Canada and Mexico. But we don't need to be importing from, and thereby supporting, unstable places around the world. We don't need to do business with people who don't like the way we think and live, who begrudge the United States her success. So if we have a $250 billion a year trade deficit just in energy, let's bring $200 billion of it home.

"ALL-OF-THE-ABOVE" ENERGY

A running theme in the 2012 presidential campaign debates was the advantages of an "all-of-the-above" energy strategy. Although Barack

Obama and Mitt Romney differed sharply on any number of policy questions, they seemed to be in general agreement on that approach. Obama put more emphasis on renewable energy, while Romney talked about renewables along with coal, gas, and shale. But the president legitimately could boast that domestic oil production had increased during his first term. Obama still has an opportunity to put that "all-of-the-above" strategy into practice, with some clarifications.

I think it's fair to say Obama's first term was more than a little confusing on energy. On the one hand, you had prominent officials in the administration taking a hard line against coal and oil. The president himself gave the order to stop offshore oil drilling after the *Deepwater Horizon* disaster. He restricted new exploration leases on federal lands. But on the other hand, the administration was claiming credit for the remarkable boom in domestic gas and oil production, even though, as Romney noted, most of that new production didn't occur on federally owned land.[6] And this administration approved the first new nuclear power plant in the United States in a generation.

Truth is, Obama and his advisers know that they've got to do nuclear power, that they can't completely kill off the coal industry, and that, as much as their supporters in Greenpeace and the Sierra Club may hate it, they would be ill-advised to put the brakes on natural gas and shale oil. Wind and solar might make sense at some point, but not as long as they require huge subsidies to make them commercially viable.

If this president wants to be remembered as the man who lifted the United States out of the Great Recession instead of presiding over a great nation's economic stagnation, he needs the jobs that a genuine "all-of-the-above" energy policy would deliver. He's got this game changer that's going to enhance the movement of manufacturing back to this country—at a time when people are becoming disenchanted with doing business in China, and at a time when Europe is going through a major crisis that it's going to be suffering from for the next ten years. Even if all Obama did was sit back and take the credit, he would be doing a tremendous service.

But at the moment, the government permitting process is imposing long delays on new development and pushing millions of jobs out a decade. If the administration adopted a more streamlined approach, we could potentially see a dramatic increase in the pace of new job creation. We have the need for jobs and we have the demand for energy—they match up beautifully. Why not move the process along?

An "all-of-the-above" energy policy goes hand in hand with building a twenty-first-century infrastructure. Natural gas–fired power plants will need new transmission lines above and below ground. Those power plants will bring electricity to new steel mills, chemical plants, and logistics hubs. There are ample job-creation opportunities for people who not only know how to build that infrastructure, but also for those with the know-how to keep it all in good working order. We can take advantage of a whole host of different skill sets that carry through to the entire economy. We need new pipelines—including the Keystone XL pipeline from Canada to the Gulf Coast that President Obama unwisely quashed—as well as new storage facilities.

Some of what I'm talking about is already happening. Nucor is building in Louisiana—as opposed to Trinidad, where we built our first DRI plant in 2006—because we were able, through a long-term agreement, to lock in our natural gas supplies for 30 years at $2 or $3 per thousand cubic feet instead of $15 or $16. Now we do not have to worry about the risk of variability in cost.

Other companies are following Nucor's lead. Voestalpine, based in Austria, is planning to build a $740 million DRI plant in Texas.[7] Methanex, a Canadian company that makes methyl alcohol and methanol-based fuels, reportedly plans to relocate a plant from Chile to Louisiana by 2014.[8] Formosa Plastics, a Taiwan-based company, is spending over $1 billion on a new plant southwest of Houston.[9] Dow Chemical is investing more than $4 billion on new facilities in Texas and around the Gulf Coast.[10] Until just a few years ago, Dow had no interest in U.S. expansion. The company was heavily invested in China. Natural gas, which Dow uses not only for power but also in its process of making plastics, makes these big moves possible.

As more U.S.-based manufacturers face the fact that China is a less-than-desirable place to do business, the lure of inexpensive energy will bring them home. But I worry that extremists within the environmentalist movement could derail progress.

Some environmentalist groups are lining up against natural gas. Now, environmentalists come in many forms, and there are extremists in any cause. But opponents of natural gas development see it as a threat to some kind of green utopia. Natural gas is supposedly dirtier than it appears, or it's "dangerous and running amok."[11] The Sierra Club's leaders have come out and said they would try and prevent new natural gas plants from being built wherever they can. The irony here is that it wasn't too long ago that the very same Sierra Club was saying natural gas is a "bridge fuel" to their preferred renewable sources of energy like solar, wind, and geothermal because natural gas doesn't emit as much CO_2 as coal and other traditional sources.[12]

Why the change of attitude? I think it might have something to do with the fact that cheap natural gas undercuts any incentive to adopt heavily subsidized renewables. Shut down the coal-fired power plants, stop natural gas power from expanding, and force everyone to find alternative energy whether it's feasible and affordable or not.

There is no rational basis for this way of thinking. *None.* The campaign to kill natural gas is anti-business, anti–free enterprise, and anti–common sense.

At the heart of the opposition to new sources of natural gas is the way the gas is extracted. The process is called hydraulic fracturing, but it's better known as fracking. It involves injecting water, sand, and other chemicals into shale under extremely high pressure to release the gas trapped inside. Fracking is a nonissue, or it should be, anyway. People have been fracking forever—since the late 1940s at least. Now that it has become more widespread and gained a higher profile, activists are trying to make an issue out of it. You know the problem with that documentary *Gasland?* It doesn't tell you that people have had flaming water long before fracking was ever invented. How do you think all of those towns called Burning Springs got their names?

All of the best evidence shows that fracking hasn't polluted groundwater or caused any other problems. The U.S. Department of Energy's National Energy Technology Laboratory, for example, released a study in 2013 finding no evidence that fracking chemicals injected deep into the ground had made their way to aquifers closer to the surface.[13] Even former Environmental Protection Agency administrator Lisa Jackson said in congressional testimony that there are no proven cases where fracking has affected water.[14]

Are there some legitimate concerns about fracking and natural gas drilling in general? Sure. Energy companies have to solve problems with wear and tear on infrastructure, noise, dust pollution, and waste management, just like any other heavy industry. Are they being addressed? In some places better than others. Far better for business and government to work together to resolve those issues than to have government needlessly clamping down because of overblown fears.

If people are worried about climate change and want to cut down carbon emissions, the country should frack *more.* In 2012, U.S. carbon emissions hit their lowest levels in 20 years, which suggests that the rapid growth of natural gas production in recent years has had no negative effect on the nation's efforts to combat global warming.[15] We've slashed emissions by as much as 500 metric tons,[16] which is about twice as much as the entire rest of the world has managed to cut since everyone climbed on the Kyoto bandwagon. The United States never ratified the Kyoto Protocol, which demanded a worldwide effort to address the threat of global warming. And we caught holy hell for it. China did ratify the treaty and spent 20 years wagging its finger at us. But as a developing country, China was exempt from most of the treaty's provisions. The Chinese now lead the world in carbon emissions.

Electricity produced from natural gas is the biggest reason America's emissions are down. Using more natural gas to make electricity means we're using considerably less coal.

COSTS AND BENEFITS

Instead of pursuing extremist policies in the name of curbing a phenomenon that is mostly beyond mankind's control, the United States should be thinking about real costs and benefits. Look at what's happening in Wyoming, Colorado, Montana, Pennsylvania, and Ohio. Better yet, look at North Dakota with its Bakken shale. They're going nuts up there. One study by IHS Consulting found that for every job in an oil or gas field, three jobs are created elsewhere in industries as diverse as manufacturing, information technology, health care, and education. Taxes and royalties are paying for schools, roads, hospitals, and research and development. The additional tax revenue alone could reach almost $1 trillion by 2035.[17]

Fact: five years ago, North Dakota produced 125,000 barrels of oil per day. By 2012, production had approached 800,000 barrels per day. Some industry experts predict North Dakota's production will reach 2 million barrels per day by the end of the decade, which would put the state on par with Nigeria, the largest oil producer in Africa and the sixth-largest producer in the world.[18]

Official unemployment in North Dakota is around 3 percent, labor participation is very high, and the average oil worker's salary is around $90,000. But the state is suffering a housing shortage, which means many well-paid welders, riggers, and electricians are sleeping in their cars or living in tents.

Did you know that just a few years ago, North Dakota was the least-visited state in America? Now, good luck finding a hotel room. What does that mean? It means there's a demand for new hotels. But they also need wider roads, new schools, new power plants, new restaurants. They need more police, more teachers, more manufacturing jobs, more construction workers. That's great. Build it and they will come. Obviously not everyone wants to move to North Dakota, so finding the right people for those jobs might be a challenge. But we've got to create a mind-set that says it's a good time to be an engineer again, it's good to be an entrepreneur. It's even good to be a welder.

North Dakota is not the only beneficiary of the shale boom. In Texas, the Eagle Ford shale formation around San Antonio has had a similar effect on the state and local economy. Although Texas is well known as an oil-producing state, Eagle Ford is a relatively recent play—and the fastest-developing natural gas region in the United States. Economists at the University of Texas at San Antonio found that in 2011, energy companies in Eagle Ford pumped out nearly $20 billion in oil and gas, created 38,000 full-time jobs, and added $10.8 billion to the regional economy. That translated to $211 million in tax revenue for San Antonio and some $312 million for the state. By 2021, economists forecast that Eagle Ford shale will generate $62.1 billion in output and more than 82,000 jobs.[19]

States that produce little or no gas and oil are beginning to see some benefits of the boom. Businesses in New York, Illinois, and South Dakota are providing important goods and services for the oil and gas supply chain. But perhaps more surprising, the one interest that has benefited *least* from the new oil and gas boom has been Big Oil. According to *Forbes,* the new American energy revolution is largely the work of about 18,000 small- and medium-sized companies.[20]

I know it isn't always obvious, but the entrepreneurial spirit still lives in the United States. It's helpful to contrast the work of tens of thousands of companies large and small, developing new and more efficient processes and better products, with the top-down efforts by almost all of the world's governments to combat global warming, which we're now calling climate change. No matter what you want to call it, those government efforts were a distraction from the looming crisis with the economy. Two decades of policies, billions of tax dollars spent, and the best we can say is that the world has reduced global carbon emissions by about 1 percent. And the economy is still lagging. Now consider this: the governments that signed on to the UN framework on climate change in 1992 could not have imagined the rise of Amazon .com, or the way Apple's iPod and iPhone would change the way people listen to music and communicate, or the emergence of companies like Tesla Motors and technologies like Google's driverless car. Private enterprise adapts quickly to changing circumstances and needs and often anticipates them. Government does not. Government can only react, and then often not very efficiently.

But nobody wants to hear that. Instead, it's just a lot of heated rhetoric about the need to do something, anything, about climate change, no matter what the cost. We would shackle ourselves to a dubious model while allowing China—mercantilist, currency-manipulating China—to operate free of any similar rules and constraints. Where's the logic? Where are the penalties? The only penalties are to us, to our job creation and our economic growth. You simply can't be a dynamic, growing economy today without having very solid energy programs and sane cost structures.

So the United States faces a choice. We could easily go the route of Mexico, which has tremendous oil and gas resources but has seen production steadily fall over the past five years because the government refuses to open exploration and development to private enterprise. We could be like Germany and start shutting down our nuclear power plants. We could embrace a point of view that opposes fossil fuel and sees natural gas as an impediment to a future of renewable energy. Or our state and federal officials could see natural gas as the gift that it is to the U.S. economy. They could facilitate and support these advances, and make sure we do energy right.

I don't mean that government should be taxing traditional sources like coal out of existence. I don't think we should be giving preferential treatment to wind or solar, either. Government should take full advantage of innovative technology instead of putting up barriers that will make the natural gas and shale oil industries less efficient. We shouldn't be picking winners and losers in the energy game. Let the market determine what's best. And right now, gas is the cheapest way to go.

We have an opportunity in this country right now to be in a unique position. With the right leadership, we can get significant economic growth going again. Build it and they will come.

TEN

WHERE THE
ROAD LEADS

Restoring American Manufacturing,

Innovation, and Competitiveness

A COUNTRY THAT DOESN'T CREATE OR MAKE OR build things is a country doomed to mediocrity. Manufacturing, and the innovation that comes with it, is indispensable to the vitality of a great nation.

It's just a fact of economic life. Manufacturing creates real wealth. Real wealth comes from innovating, making, and building things. It's a process that reinforces itself and reinvents itself; moves forward, not sideways; and does not stray from its core to extremes. And it lasts. Manufacturing has always benefited the U.S. economy. Always.

Economists point out that, of all industries, manufacturing has the largest multiplier effect. Every dollar of activity in the business of creating and making things creates an additional $1.34 in activity in the broader economy. The only other sector that comes close is construction—the business of building things—which generates about 97 cents in the economy for every dollar.

Given all of the benefits of manufacturing, it's heartbreaking to see how the sector has declined from 25 percent of the nation's economy in the 1960s[1] to around 12 percent today.[2] The nation has seen 79 percent

FIGURE 10.1   ECONOMIC MULTIPLIER OF THE MANUFACTURING SECTOR

Every dollar of activity in manufacturing creates an additional $1.34 in economic activity in the general economy, more than any other sector

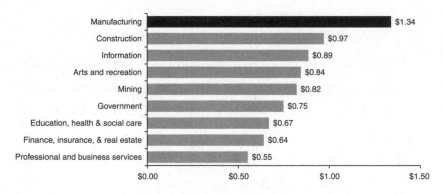

Source: *New America Foundation, "Value Added: America's Manufacturing," April 8, 2012, http://newamerica.net/publications/policy/value_added_americas_manu facturing_future.*

of America's total manufacturing—15 of 19 distinct sectors—decline sharply between 2000 and 2009. More than 5 million well-paying manufacturing jobs have disappeared just since 2000. Only 12 million Americans continue to work in manufacturing today.[3]

The story of the past half century has been one of rejecting and replacing sound principles with phony economics principles, phony idealism, and a phony ethic that elevated thieving, stealing, and cheating to cardinal virtues.

Five years after the housing bubble burst and Wall Street was brought to its knees, it should be clear that we've lost sight of how to create real wealth. Service industries—bankers, insurers, lawyers, doctors, accountants—thrive when the core economy is strong. The manufacturing sector supports another 6 million jobs in services, including transportation and logistics, wholesaling, accounting and finance, and the legal services sector.[4] Put simply, taking one thing and making something more from it, something of real value, has always been better than trying to conjure something from nothing.

We let special interests get too big, and we let unions get out of control. We allowed government regulations to become so onerous that American businesses began looking to other countries—ones that made promises that were too good to be true—for better opportunities. We allowed the number-one jobs killer, currency manipulation, to gain an upper hand and give predatory foreign competitors massive cost advantages over us. And with every recession, recovery has become more difficult. The Great Recession was the culmination of nearly 60 years of worshipping false economic idols and chasing illusions. As a wise man once said, we cannot escape history.

I know many Americans who've lost hope. I know people who look at the economic landscape and say, "Well, that's it. Game over." That kind of fatalism isn't helpful. No problem is unsolvable. It's time to de-emphasize the extremes and return to the fundamentals of creating, innovating, making, and building things. It's the only road that leads back to full employment in the United States, and it's the path Nucor has been following for almost 50 years. Nucor and companies like ours have created real wealth, not phony bubble wealth.

ACCELERATING A MANUFACTURING RENAISSANCE

If the United States is going to escape the cycle of bubbles and resolve its systemic economic problems, the nation must choose to close the national infrastructure deficit and cultivate an energy revolution with natural gas as the road to travel.

Short-term fixes won't cut it anymore. Even through the current gloom, we can see rays of hope for an honest-to-goodness American manufacturing resurgence. The automotive industry is coming back strong, and we're seeing encouraging signs of life along the Gulf Coast, from Texas to Florida. But without other fundamental reforms, this fledgling renaissance won't last.

I realize that *industrial* is a dirty word in America. But I also know that every other developed country in the world has a manufacturing strategy. They all coordinate tax, trade, and other policies. Japan's Ministry of Economy, Trade and Industry is the example most university economics professors love to cite. France and Germany have strong industrial policies, too.

Then there's China. The Chinese set specific production targets, and they use tax revenue to subsidize industries to reach their goals. They closely monitor progress and penalize laggards along the way. You really don't want to miss a production target in China.

I'm not saying we should be creating new bureaucracies or making five-year industrial plans. If anything, we have too much bureaucracy in this country right now. But let's face facts: the world says one thing about open markets and free trade but does another. Whatever sharp cultural or political or language differences may separate the Japanese from the Chinese, or the Germans from the French, this much they all have in common: they know how to advance and protect their economic interests. I think we could do a much better job of advancing and protecting our own interests. That, in a nutshell, is the basis of a bona fide American industrial policy.

In principle, any industrial policy would begin by saying the business of creating, making, and building things must be at the heart of any overarching economic strategy. With a concerted national effort aimed at creating manufacturing jobs, we could boost the number of people working in the industry from 12 million to 20 million or 25 million in the next ten years.[5] An American industrial policy would help U.S. businesses, or at least not put them at a disadvantage, in the global marketplace. An American industrial policy should promote U.S. exports, attract foreign direct investment in our industries, retrain our unemployed workers to build on the skills they already have, and unleash private-sector innovation. But an industrial policy should insist that while business leaders may certainly profit from operations overseas, they mustn't do so at the expense of the American economy, the American workforce, and future generations of Americans.

I think any American industrial policy needs to place much greater emphasis on producers than consumers. I think experts obsess a little too much about what's good for the American consumer. The whole free-trade ideology revolves around the supposed benefits for the consumer. "We can't have tariffs! Think of what that would do to the consumer!" Fear of what might happen to the consumer is just that: a fear. And even if it's a legitimate worry, the crisis we're trying to resolve is worse than the sum of all those fears. The consumer cannot be the be-all, end-all. If I feed myself ice cream 24 hours a day, is that good for me as an ice-cream consumer? It might seem that way until I get sick and drop dead.

Before you can be a consumer, you must first be a producer. Of course, you can also consume if you're on the dole. A lot of people do. But since putting everyone on the government's tab isn't what this country is about, our objective should be to make a nation of producers and contributors, people who add value to the society. Call them self-governing citizens if you like. The point is, you have to be a producer before you earn the right to be a consumer.

I like to use the example of buying a T-shirt. People love paying $5 or $10 for a T-shirt made in China or Malaysia or wherever. If I have $20 in my pocket, I can buy a shirt, a caffè latte at the coffee shop, and some laundry detergent to get the coffee stains out later. Paying so little for T-shirts is a fine thing, as long as the people buying them here are paying for them with money they've earned from a job, preferably a well-paying one.

Well, what happens if you're not working? Or what happens if you're making minimum wage flipping burgers? In that case, you don't have $20 to spend on cheap T-shirts and laundry detergent. Then you're just trying to pay the rent and put some gas in the tank. Suddenly, it doesn't matter if the T-shirt is $10, or $5, or even $1. You can't afford it.

I don't want to oversimplify too much, but what's true of people is true of countries in this case. When the United States cedes its real wealth–producing power to foreign countries in the name of free trade, or on the basis of some bogus theory that says we can simply service the global economy and still be rich, we're going to end up just like the poor burger flipper struggling to pay his rent.

What we really want is people investing and manufacturing in the United States because of the multiplier effect it would bring to the economy. Remember: $1 of manufacturing means $1.34 for the total economy. Then it doesn't matter if you're paying $10 or even $20 for a T-shirt. People can afford it either way.

Easier said than done, I realize. Because in order to move from the dysfunctional economic model we have today to a model that restores real wealth creation, there will be some pain. Before we're in balance, the consumer may end up paying $15 for a T-shirt instead of $10 or $5. We're going to have to live with that for a while as we rebuild a healthy economy by rebuilding manufacturing.

GOVERNMENT AND BUSINESS
SHOULDN'T BE ANTAGONISTS

An American industrial policy assumes government and business will work together with some degree of harmony. But aren't government and business too close as it is? What's the difference between government policy that encourages private enterprise at home and abroad versus one that's out-and-out crony capitalism?

Truth is, the relationship between the private and public sector right now is a lot more complicated than most Americans realize. When government regulates business, it's in the business's interest to make sure government doesn't regulate too much. Problems start when lobbyists jockey for special favors and exceptions. Larger businesses can afford better lobbyists than small businesses can. It's ugly.

Government should not pick winners and losers. An American industrial policy would say to manufacturers: make it here to sell it here first. Do business where you know you'll have the rule of law, not government by bribery and kickbacks; where you have the world's best intellectual property protection; where you have a highly skilled workforce; and where you have a well-developed infrastructure. We can make that happen. Above all, the role of government in a globally competitive world is to create an environment where everyone can produce on a level playing field. Create the incentives, step back, and let business find a way to be competitive.

What government shouldn't do is put anchors on businesses or people. If you're fast and in good shape, you're going to beat the slow, fat guy every day of the week. If you're smart, you'll outwit the dummy. It isn't the role of government to step in and say, "We're going to compensate for the fact that you're fat, slow, and can't put two and two together." How would government do that fairly? When you try to put chains on people, they'll figure out a way to be competitive somewhere else.

Environmental regulations put a significant drag on economic recovery and expansion. Earlier, I detailed some of the extreme measures that the federal government has taken to clamp down on pollution and greenhouse gases. Other countries don't have the stringent rules we have. China's environmental protections are paper-thin. That puts us at a massive disadvantage.

I can anticipate the objection, which is often something along the lines of, "What are you saying, DiMicco? You want to repeal the Clean Water Act and the Clean Air Act and bring back acid rain?" For the record, no, I do not want to repeal the Clean Water Act or Clean Air Act, and I'm not a fan of acid rain. I'm not in favor of turning back the clock 30 or 40 years. But that's not where the discussion is today, anyway. When we talk about environmental regulations in 2014 we're often talking about whether it's absolutely necessary to add another multi-billion-dollar burden to industry by tweaking the emissions standards on certain fine particles, defined as 2.5 micrometers and smaller. Do the costs outweigh the benefits? Well, maybe not when businesses close up shop because they can't afford to pass the compliance costs on to their customers anymore. The air may be microscopically cleaner, but only because nobody's working!

Delayed permitting and unfettered litigation also hurts manufacturing and slows down recovery. Nucor's adventure in Louisiana shows how tough it can be to build a new facility even in a business-friendly state. If a business spends thousands, or in some instances millions, of dollars submitting to a state and federal environmental review process, only to be sued by a third party after completing the process successfully, that's not really an incentive to build. The whole purpose of a permit is for the government to ensure before the fact that a project won't have an undue environmental impact. I think any decent American industrial policy would include regulatory reforms that put reasonable limits on redundant permitting and the right to sue.

Sure, there are certain things government has got to do. Government needs to make sure monopolies don't distort the market. Government can set basic standards to make sure people don't get rooked. But aside from that, a healthy economy encourages people to go into business because they can make a living at it; they can invest their money and get a return that makes sense to them.

Another way to unchain the U.S. economy would be to fix a badly out-of-date, anti-competitive tax system. Today, the United States has the highest corporate tax rate of any industrialized nation, at 39.1 percent. The former leader, Japan, cut its corporate rate to 37 percent in 2013 from 39.5 percent. The average corporate tax rate among the 38 members of the Organization for Economic Cooperation and Development is 25 percent. If a business is deciding where to locate, the tax burden may not be the sole consideration, but it is an important one. If the tax rate is nearly 40 percent in the United States and 20 percent in China, obviously that's just one more reason to move to China. Low corporate tax rates also explain why a lot of U.S. corporations create

FIGURE 10.2 TAX RATES BY COUNTRY

At 40%, the US has the highest corporate tax rate in the OECD, but still collects less revenues as percentage of GDP compared to other advanced economies

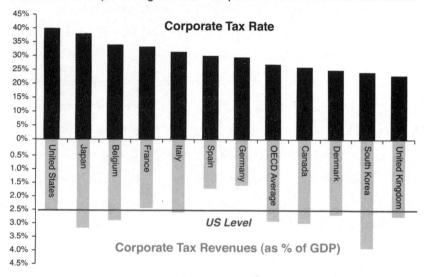

Source: *"Revenue Statistics—Comparative Tables," OECD Statistical Database, http://stats.oecd.org/Index.aspx?DataSetCode=REV; OECD Tax Database, OECD, http://www.oecd.org/tax/tax-policy/tax-database.htm#C_CorporateCaptial.*

subsidiaries in places like Ireland, Switzerland, and Luxembourg. Most of the time, these are nothing more than a post office box.

Our tax code right now is loaded with loopholes and exceptions that give companies incentives to offshore jobs. It's absurd. Why did Japan cut its corporate tax rate? Easy—to be more competitive. We need to compete with that. The ideal U.S. corporate tax rate would be 23 percent. According to a Milken Institute study, such a cut would boost the nation's GDP by $282 billion and increase employment by 1.83 million.[6] I think the only thing holding Congress back from cutting the corporate rate is this false perception that tax cuts are a gift to the corporations. What they need to understand is that the gift would be repaid, many times over, with lower unemployment and higher growth. An American industrial policy could also use the tax code to give businesses incentives to provide vocational training and fund continuing education and hire the long-term unemployed.

We can have a healthy economic environment where government supports a free-enterprise system and supports large and small businesses to be globally competitive. But if you want to encourage people to go into business and you think that government's got all the answers, you risk distorting the system from the get-go. Any business worth getting into—large or small—should be worth getting into without government subsidizing it.

SIGNS OF A RENAISSANCE

Why are some U.S. companies choosing to come back to America? In March 2013, Google announced it would manufacture its highly anticipated Google Glass in California, though continue to source the device's parts from Asia. Google didn't decide to build the wearable computer because of any subsidies the federal or state government may be offering. There are none. Google, like other companies, is coming home because they can better control their intellectual property, and because the revolution in energy is improving America's comparative advantage.

It's pretty basic economics. A new wave of technological innovation—3-D printing is another example of this—is making it easier, cheaper, and faster for American companies to design and build in the United States rather than halfway around the globe. Every day, there's something new. But companies are also coming back because of a growing disenchantment with China. Some of these companies say the cost of shipping is starting to cut into their savings on labor. There's more to it than a simple cost-saving calculation. Many small businesses and entrepreneurs are discovering, often too late, that there's no real quality control over there.

Consider the case of Sleek Audio, a small business that makes iPod accessories. Mark Krywko and his son, Jason, started their company near St. Petersburg, Florida in 2007. They shopped around several U.S. manufacturers before going with the lowest bidder—a factory in China's Guangdong Province. In 2011, the Krywkos decided to bring their manufacturing back home. What changed? They got fed up with too many shipping delays, too much travel, and rising costs. The final straw was a ruined shipment of 10,000 sets of earphones that nearly bankrupted the company. "It became very difficult and taxing on us," Jason told *Fortune* magazine. "Now we control the quality of the product. No more waiting for production has been a wonderful thing."[7]

China's quality-control problem is also a health problem. News stories in recent years about lead paint in children's toys, flammable clothing, and poisoned pet food have forced millions of consumers to pay closer attention to what they buy. People are learning that just because an American brand name is on the box, that doesn't automatically mean what's inside meets a higher American standard.

Another reason companies are abandoning China and Asia more widely: the need for strong copyright and patent protections. Despite repeated promises of better enforcement, counterfeiting and piracy remain rampant in Asia, costing U.S. firms an estimated $250 billion a year. And it isn't just CDs and movies. It's computer chips, smartphones, and appliances. *USA Today* profiled the case of Farouk Systems, which until a few years ago was making women's hair irons and hair dryers in South Korea and China. According to CEO Farouk Shami, the company was spending $500,000 battling counterfeiters. He finally decided to move his manufacturing operations to a factory in Houston that employs about 1,000 workers. Even though costs are about 30 percent lower in China, Shami says the "Made in the USA" stamp on his products will boost sales.[8]

For all of those reasons, we're seeing a flow of manufacturing back to the United States. Could the bloom be coming off the rose? Can this trend be sped up?

We've got to get a handle on our $475 billion trade deficit. And the way to do that is to make sure our foreign competitors are held to the same standards that we hold ourselves. If a country wants access to our markets and agrees to act a certain way, we'd better hold them to their word.

More than anything else, what we need is clarity and resolve. Our trade policy has got to say that while we may be free traders, we're not idiots. We won't do business with any country that does not practice rules-based free trade, and we intend to hold those countries accountable at the World Trade Organization (WTO) when possible but unilaterally if necessary. If a country manipulates its currency and gets a 25 percent advantage, then we need to impose a 25 percent tax on every last widget that enters the United States from that country until the manipulation stops. It's only fair.

If we believe in free enterprise, if we say we believe in free trade, and we believe that the best team wins, then we've got to take the steps that help us to be the best team. Being the best team doesn't mean cheating. So if other people are cheating, we've got to use every means at our disposal to undo their ability to cheat. But we've got a big hole to dig out of. Economist Ian Fletcher points out in *Free Trade Doesn't Work: What Should Replace it and Why* that Americans have bought roughly $6 trillion more in foreign goods over the past 20 years than we've sold. "If the U.S. were a developing country," Fletcher writes, "our deficits would have reached the five percent level that the International Monetary Fund takes as a benchmark of a financial crisis."[9] Yet the federal government has done little to reverse the deficit. The problem is a structural defect that policy makers allowed to get worse over time. I hear a lot of lip service from politicians about the need for more exports. That's great. Who is going to argue with that? The problem is, as I've said time and again, we let our foreign competitors get away with distorting the system we built after World War II. That needs to be corrected if the manufacturing renaissance I've described is going to come to fruition.

Now, I've been arguing that we could solve at least half of the trade deficit problem simply by using the resources sitting directly under our feet. If we could meet the domestic demand for cheap energy by tapping the resources we've already got, the United States could cut upward of $300 billion from our annual trade imbalance.[10] We wouldn't have to import oil from Saudi Arabia anymore. We would replace the Saudis as the largest oil exporter on earth. We could do it. But when we talk about enforcing rules-based trade, that means we need to go after other countries that use energy subsidies to give their exports a leg up. We're not going to subsidize energy here because we wouldn't want them subsidizing energy over there. Low-cost energy is vital to manufacturing, but it cannot be subsidized. Those are the rules. From that standpoint, whether it's tax breaks or subsidies or free energy, when it costs American companies billions in energy costs, while a foreign competitor is paying less than that or nothing at all, that's obviously a distortion that needs correcting. If China is subsidizing energy for its exporters, then the United States needs to seek penalties so that when those goods land on U.S. soil, those exports don't unfairly benefit from that subsidy.

Manufactured goods compose the other half of the deficit equation. Again, the reason China can vastly undersell us is that they've pegged their currency to our dollar at a level much lower than the market rate. Weaker foreign currencies also make U.S. goods more expensive to import, which only exacerbates our deficit.

It's scandalous how much the U.S. government has slacked off in its pursuit of countervailing and anti-dumping duties in recent years. We're too passive. If all we did was return to the level of enforcement we had a decade ago, we could create up to 400,000 jobs.[11]

The effect of cheating on the U.S. manufacturing base is compelling. Since the WTO took effect and China gained admission in 1999, the United States has lost around 6 million manufacturing jobs.[12] When you consider the multiplier effect manufacturing has on other industries, the job losses are even larger. Job growth has been so slow after each successive recession because distortions like this are allowed to continue and drive jobs away permanently. We don't get a rebound in job growth when the economy improves because people aren't coming back from being laid off.

FIGURE 10.3   ANTI-DUMPING INITIATIONS SINCE 1999

A former leader in enforcing trade policies, the United States has
fallen behind all its major trading partners

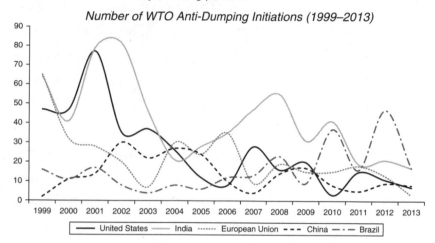

Number of WTO Anti-Dumping Initiations (1999–2013)

Source: *World Trade Organization, "Anti-dumping Initiations: By Reporting Member
01/01/1995–31/12/2013," http://www.wto.org/english/tratop_e/adp_e/AD_Initiations
ByRepMem.pdf.*

The Chinese are smart. They understand that as long as they can
get away with their predatory, mercantilist trade practices, they're going
to. But they also understand that once they're called on it—and I don't
mean chiding them in a diplomatically worded speech by the president
or the secretary of commerce at some state dinner or G8 summit—then
they'll have to stop. International pressure has nudged China a little,
but nowhere near the yuan's total undervaluation of 30 to 40 percent.
The truth is, they need us as much as we need them. But because we've
let them get away with cheating for so long, they keep cheating. Once

they're forced to abide by international trade rules, they'll stop—just like the Germans and Japanese did. China's not going cut off its thumb because of a hangnail.

It should go without saying that China isn't the only offender when it comes to currency manipulation. But it's the biggest. Thailand, South Korea, Japan, the European Union, and even Switzerland influence their currencies to some extent. And it's no wonder. If one country cheats and gets away with it, they all cheat—otherwise they'll find themselves in America's predicament. I can tell you that cheating has had a terrible effect on the U.S. steel industry. Steel is a particularly egregious case because China's steel production went from 100 million tons to 700 million tons in a matter of seven or eight years.[13] And the Chinese have shamelessly dumped steel in the United States, selling their steel plate below cost. How did they pull it off when they have to import energy and raw materials, and then export the finished product at $40 a ton when we can do it for a fraction of the cost? Dishonestly. The only way it makes sense is if Chinese steel is heavily subsidized. It's simply impossible otherwise.

If China wants to subsidize goods and services at home, who are we to object? The Chinese can create jobs that way, if they want. But turn those subsidies into an export machine, and it's not only wrong, it's illegal. Unfortunately, the United States hasn't been consistent about using international institutions like the WTO to enforce the rules. That needs to change. We need to step up our trade enforcement efforts in the WTO, and we need to make better use of the U.S. Trade Representative, our chief trade negotiator. We shouldn't be shy about using bilateral and multilateral negotiations, either.

WHAT GOOD CAN INSTITUTIONS DO?

You need accountability. That said, private enterprise cannot effectively fight foreign governments on trade disputes. Nucor, for example, cannot file an illegal steel dumping complaint with the WTO based on currency manipulation. We've tried to get the federal government to recognize currency manipulation as a subsidy, but we haven't been successful. We'll keep trying to persuade our political leaders that we're right, because the truth is, any answer to our foreign-trade imbalance requires a government-to-government solution.

I had the honor of serving on the U.S. Manufacturing Council, a group of 25 people from the private sector, mostly CEOs and COOs, appointed by the U.S. commerce secretary to offer advice on policies that affect the industry. I served on the council under Presidents Bush and Obama, from 2008 to 2011. It was an interesting experience, but it also showed me just how dysfunctional the government can be on the trade question. To be honest, one of the more frustrating aspects of the appointment was running into bureaucrats from various departments and federal agencies that took a rather parochial view of their responsibilities. A lot of times the answer to a question about currency manipulation or dumping or countervailing duties tended to be "You need to talk to somebody else about that."

I remember one meeting with Commerce Department officials where one of my fellow CEOs argued how one of the biggest impediments to the revival of U.S.-based manufacturing is Chinese currency manipulation. The response: "Well, that's a Treasury Department issue. We don't get into that." I wasn't too happy with that answer. But that's the answer we get all the time. It doesn't work. It doesn't do us any good to say 50 percent of the problem is currency manipulation, and the other 50 percent is lax enforcement of international trade agreements, if nobody is on the same page and everyone guards their own little fiefdoms. What happens is, the Commerce Department defers to the Treasury Department, and the Treasury Department defers to multinational corporations. There is concern in our government about how China behaves with respect to our debt. Maybe they don't sell it. Maybe they don't buy anymore. Or maybe we're letting fear get in the way of sound policy. In any case, we need much better coordination to support rules-based free trade and global competition.

If we're really serious about manufacturing in this country and we realize there are complex policy components—energy, trade, taxes—then we need to be able to cross departmental lines of responsibility. I don't think we need to create yet another cabinet-level department. The Obama administration set up the Interagency Trade Enforcement Center, which isn't a new department but rather a coordinated effort of the U.S. Trade Representative and the Department of Commerce. Its purpose is to bring together all of the groups and agencies involved with enforcing U.S. trade rights. That's a step in the right direction. That could bring the level of coordination, which we don't really have now, closer to where it needs to be.

FOSTERING MORE INNOVATION

Promoting innovation is the final component of a new American industrial policy. The United States today still leads the world in research and development spending. But the country is in danger of losing ground to China and the European Union if we decide to stand pat. And an even bigger risk is losing the ability to innovate entirely, as manufacturers offshore their research and development operations in the same way they offshored their fabrication and assembly operations.

Congress could help recharge American innovators by making the R&D tax credit permanent instead of continuing to let it expire and then reinstating it retroactively. The tax credit frees up between $5 billion and $10 billion a year for businesses to invest in cutting-edge research.[14] And, unlike a subsidy, tax credits give businesses the flexibility to invest based on what the market demands, not what a federal agency decrees.

Obviously, there's more than one way to innovate. There's innovation that takes place on an incremental basis, there's game-changing innovation, and there are degrees in between. Nucor has focused on all of it. We are focused on being able to take risks on game-changing technology that no one else is willing to take. And our strong financial position allowed us to do that without being so overly fearful of failure that we didn't act when opportunities arose. Time and again, whether it was expanding into cold-rolled sheet metal or forming a partnership with Yamato Steel to produce large construction girders or acquiring companies like Auburn Steel and Birmingham Steel, we knew we could take the risks and knew we could not only survive but also thrive if the investments paid off.

We have taken advantage of game-changing technologies from day one. We had the electric-arc furnace. None of the big, integrated steelmakers used that technology, which had only been around for maybe

20 years when Nucor saw a way of using it to compete effectively in the steel joist market. But we've also recognized the importance of incremental innovation on whatever process that we start out with. Direct reduced iron (DRI) is an example. The process has been around for years. The problem was it didn't produce a really high-quality scrap substitute. It didn't make sense for us to use DRI until we needed a stable alternative to surplus scrap metal as a raw material, and only then after our engineering team in Trinidad figured out how to make much higher-quality DRI pellets.

But a business—or a nation—cannot survive on game-changing technology for very long, unless there is a vision of innovation that is more mundane, more incremental. Every once in a while, incremental changes can have game-changing effects. That's why as a business, we're always looking to do things more efficiently, more productively, safer, and at a lower cost. Our goal is to progress, to reward our people for great performance, and to seize opportunities when they arise. We're never satisfied with sitting still.

I like to use the analogy of a mountain climber. At Nucor, we're going up a mountain that has no top. We're not focused on getting to the top of the mountain. We can't be. If you're focused on getting to the top of the mountain, once you get there where do you go? Down. Our entire mentality, our culture—the culture Ken Iverson began building 50 years ago—is one of continued improvement. At Nucor we say that we are on a journey up a mountain without a top. Frankly, that's why Nucor has been able to overtake older, more established companies. Almost all of them had put limitations on themselves. The Bethlehems and Republics of the world only thought of themselves as steel producers using blast furnaces, coke ovens, and unionized shops. At Nucor, we never put those limitations on our business. We're a steel company and a technology company and an engineering company and a recycling company. Maybe decades from now, we'll be another kind of company. But the important thing is, we're a profitable company.

The other guys said, "Hey, if I do that, I've got to throw away everything I've already done"—not realizing, of course, that it isn't true and that if they didn't seize new opportunities themselves, someone else would.

You can't be that way. You constantly have to be looking for a better way. You can't be satisfied with the status quo. And when you have an energized team that takes ownership of that type of philosophy and recognizes they're going to have opportunities come their way based upon how they perform and how they work together as a team, then innovation becomes a kind of self-fulfilling prophecy. It's a constant battle to make sure that we stay true to that ethos, as opposed to getting fat, dumb, and happy.

A PHILOSOPHY OF RISK AND
DOING WHAT'S RIGHT

The philosophy that guided Nucor's growth and success over the past 50 years can also guide the United States in the coming decades. It's a quintessentially American vision for the country—far-sighted, progressive, with shared sacrifice and shared prosperity.

What made America great? It was an optimistic belief in the possible tempered by a practical understanding of man's limits. Mostly, though, it was about taking risks. Try to imagine the United States becoming a great power if the Environmental Protection Agency or the Consumer Product Safety Commission existed 200 years ago.

I think a lot about our country's history and future in the context of Nucor's history and future. We're the biggest steel company in America. How did we get that way? When Ken Iverson brought Nucor into the steel business in the 1960s, the corporation was fighting for its very survival. It's fair to say Nucor had a bet-the-company philosophy when all Iverson had were two fabricating plants making steel joists. There wasn't a whole lot to lose. And the potential reward for Iverson was not to grow into the largest steel producer in the country, but simply to get control of the company's destiny so he could operate the other businesses profitably instead of being at the mercy of uncooperative suppliers.

There was a lot more to lose when Nucor got into the slab-casting, cold-rolled sheet business in Indiana in the 1980s because we were a much bigger company by then. But we also had a business model: have a strong balance sheet; don't spend more than you make; keep that balance sheet strong so that you can take risks and build new plants; take on new technologies; and don't lose the company because of it.

If you stop and think about it, the United States grew from a tiny collection of independent British colonies into the greatest nation the world has ever seen in much the same way: through fiscal discipline, prudent investments, "internal improvements," expanding territory, risk taking, and innovation, all while remaining faithful to the nation's founding principles.

We've gotten off track. But that doesn't mean we can't get back on it. We could choose to be a country in decline. Or we could regain control of our country's destiny. The world still looks to the United States as a leader in commerce and in freedom. But you cannot be a leader in anything if you're not optimistic. That doesn't mean that you're not a realist about the challenges and the risks that are out there. I'm just a firm believer that we can get back on track. We can take something that's going in the wrong direction and, by focusing on the fundamentals and having an optimistic view of the future, we can turn it around. I'm unwilling to accept any foregone conclusion that we are doomed. We need to fight.

It's very clear what we should do: build public-private partnerships to restore the manufacturing base, rebuild the nation's infrastructure, develop our natural resources, level the playing field of international trade, revitalize the middle class, and put 30 million Americans to work. Any government policy that doesn't support those things needs to be scrapped. It's that simple.

I think the American people will rise to the occasion, but it takes leadership. Nothing happens by accident. Every now and then, we need certain people to come along and help us understand where we need to go. The very best leaders show the way and empower people to take it upon themselves to get there.

No problem is unsolvable. Every crisis requires resolution. I'll tell you something that I haven't often discussed publicly. Nucor could have very easily fallen to pieces in 2000. Ken Iverson had retired in 1997. He had been ill for a long time and passed away in 2002. Losing our founder was very tough. The leadership transition wasn't easy. A lot of people wondered, with good reason, whether the Nucor culture would die with Ken. There was a lot of uncertainty.

When the board named me CEO in 2000, I made sure to assemble a team—and I do mean a *team*—that had an optimistic vision. I cannot take credit. Without the team, we would have failed. And as the steel industry was in turmoil with 32 companies in bankruptcy and the world was seemingly falling apart, where was Nucor? Climbing the mountain without a top, taking advantage of every opportunity to be in a better place tomorrow than we were the day before.

I say where Nucor was in 2000 is no different than where the country is today. Are we on the wrong track? Yes. Let's change tracks. But if you don't believe it can be done, it won't get done. If you doubt yourself and the ability of the country to succeed, the project will founder. I guarantee we won't succeed if we can't trust each other to do right, and if all our fractured political leadership can do is undermine the other side and settle into extreme positions. Congress is frozen. The fiscal cliff deal raised taxes in a way that actually punishes investment and small businesses. It took Congress four years to finally pass a budget. The divisiveness bothers me. It should bother everyone.

In any free society, we're going to have disagreements. But we're at a point where our disagreements are undermining the social and economic structure of the nation. It's frustrating to see where we are now compared to where we could be if we had dealt with the jobs crisis right away in 2009 and 2010. You can't ignore crises and get your house in order economically, whether it's from a debt standpoint or from a growth standpoint. We're supposed to be better than this. We have a unique opportunity to govern ourselves and take hold of our own futures through the beautiful system we have in place. But it takes people articulating the difference between what's right and what's wrong, and giving Americans a positive vision for the future.

We don't need government to save us from ourselves. We merely need government to give us the tools, the resources, the education, and the opportunity to succeed. That's what Nucor has always been about. You hire the right people and put them in place with the best tools and the best training. Then get out of the way.

The rest will take care of itself.

NOTES

INTRODUCTION

1. David L. Fortney, "The Little Steel Mill That Could," *Reader's Digest,* August 1985.
2. Ruth Simon, "Nucor's Boldest Gamble," *Forbes,* April 3, 1989.
3. Dumping is the practice of selling imported products at a price below the cost of production or the market price.

CHAPTER 1

1. Bureau of Labor Statistics, Current Population Survey, http://www.bls.gov /cps/.
2. Gerald F. Seib, "In Crisis, Opportunity for Obama," *Wall Street Journal,* November 21, 2008, http://online.wsj.com/news/articles/SB122721278056345271.
3. Bureau of Labor Statistics, Current Employment Statistics, http://www.bls.gov /ces/.
4. Bureau of Labor Statistics, Current Population Survey, http://www.bls.gov /cps/.
5. Jack Welch, Twitter post, October 5, 2012, 5:35 am, https://twitter.com/jack _welch.
6. Jack Welch, Twitter post, October 4, 2012, 8:02 pm, https://twitter.com/jack _welch.
7. "Real Unemployment," or the U6 rate, is defined by the Bureau of Labor Statistics as total unemployed, plus all marginally attached workers plus total employed part time for economic reasons. Bureau of Labor Statistics, Current Population Survey, http://www.bls.gov/cps/.
8. Bureau of Labor Statistics, Current Population Survey, http://www.bls.gov /cps/.
9. Dean Baker and Kevin Hassett, "The Human Disaster of Unemployment," *New York Times,* May 12, 2012, http://www.nytimes.com/2012/05/13/opinion/sun day/the-human-disaster-of-unemployment.html?pagewanted=1.

10. Bureau of Labor Statistics, Current Employment Statistics, http://www.bls.gov /ces/. Proprietary analysis by Garten Rothkopf.

CHAPTER 2

1. John F. Kennedy, "Moon Speech," Houston, Texas, September 12, 1962, John F. Kennedy Presidential Library and Museum, http://www.jfklibrary.org/Asset -Viewer/MkATdOcdU06X5uNHbmqm1Q.aspx.
2. Ibid.
3. Ibid.

CHAPTER 3

1. Frank Newport, "Americans Unsure If Best Times for U.S. Are Past or to Come," *Gallup*, January 2, 2013, http://www.gallup.com/poll/159596/ameri cans-unsure-best-times-past.aspx.
2. Louis D. Johnston, "History Lessons: Understanding the Decline in Manu-facturing," *MinnPost*, February 22, 2012, http://www.minnpost.com/macro -micro-minnesota/2012/02/history-lessons-understanding-decline-manufac turing#sourcenote.
3. "A Country Study: Japan," Federal Research Service Library of Congress, http:// lcweb2.loc.gov/frd/cs/jptoc.html.
4. FRED (Federal Reserve Economic Data), "Germany/U.S. Foreign Exchange Rate," Federal Reserve Bank of St. Louis, 2014, http://research.stlouisfed.org /fred2/series/EXGEUS?cid=277.
5. FRED (Federal Reserve Economic Data), "Japan/U.S. Foreign Exchange Rate," Federal Reserve Bank of St. Louis, 2014, http://research.stlouisfed.org/fred2 /series/EXJPUS.
6. "U.S. Trade in Goods and Services-Balance of Payments (BOP) Basis," U.S. Census Bureau, June 4, 2014, http://www.census.gov/foreign-trade/statistics /historical/gands.pdf.
7. Ibid.
8. "IMF Country Report No. 14/235 PEOPLE'S REPUBLIC OF CHINA," Inter-national Monetary Fund, July 2014, http://www.imf.org/external/pubs/ft/scr /2014/cr14235.pdf.
9. Robert E. Scott, "Revaluing China's Currency Could Boost US Economic Recov-ery," Economic Policy Institute, June 17, 2011, http://www.epi.org/publication /revaluing_chinas_currency_could_boost_us_economic_recovery/.
10. William J. Clinton, "Letter to Congress Advocating Granting China Permanent Normal Trade Relations," Office of the Press Secretary, March 8, 2000, http:// china.usc.edu/(S(4h00e555weg0rxfp21g4ef55)A(gL3jyH-YzgEkAAAAMjNi OTQ2YzAtNDVmZS00ZDc1LWFhODEtNmNjNGQ5OGRkZWVjz3PFvzPFL m_eezPTWjdBJqZvZow1))/ShowArticle.aspx?articleID=3058&AspxAutoDete ctCookieSupport=1.

11. William J. Clinton, "The President's News Conference," Online by Gerhard Peters and John T. Woolley, *The American Presidency Project*, March 29, 2000, http://www.presidency.ucsb.edu/ws/?pid=58305.

CHAPTER 4

1. Elizabeth Warren, Democratic National Convention Speech, Charlotte, North Carolina, September 5, 2012, http://www.politico.com/news/stories/09 12/80802.html.
2. "U.S. Trade in Goods and Services-Balance of Payments (BOP) Basis," U.S. Census Bureau, June 4, 2014, http://www.census.gov/foreign-trade/statistics/his torical/gands.pdf.

CHAPTER 5

1. Bureau of Labor Statistics, Current Population Survey, http://www.bls.gov /cps/.
2. Bureau of Labor Statistics, Current Employment Statistics, http://www.bls.gov /ces/.
3. Bureau of Labor Statistics, Current Population Survey.
4. Dan DiMicco, "Buy American," interview by Leslie Stahl, *60 Minutes,* CBS, February 15, 2009.
5. Michael Lind, "America is Losing the Trade War," *Salon*, September 28, 2010, http://www.salon.com/2010/09/28/lind_america_trade_war/.
6. Bureau of Economic Analysis, "Value Added by Industry as a Percentage of Gross Domestic Product," November 13, 2012, http://www.bea.gov/industry/gdpby ind_data.htm.
7. Robert E. Scott, "Trading Away the Manufacturing Advantage," Economic Policy Institute, September 30, 2013, http://www.epi.org/publication/trading -manufacturing-advantage-china-trade/.
8. Adam Smith, *An Inquiry into the Nature and Causes of the Wealth of Nations*, 1776.
9. "Certain Oil Country Tubular Goods from China Injure U.S. Industry, Says USITC," USITC, December 30, 2009, http://usitc.gov/press_room/news_releas e/2009/er1230gg1.htm.

CHAPTER 6

1. President Barack Obama, Weekly Address, August 1, 2009, http://www.white house.gov/the-press-office/weekly-address-president-obama-says-gdp-num bers-show-recovery-act-working-long-term.
2. Gary Locke, Remarks at National Advisory Council on Innovation and Entrepreneurship Forum, Chapel Hill, North Carolina, March 15, 2011, http:// www.commerce.gov/news/secretary-speeches/2011/03/15/remarks-national -advisory-council-innovation-and-entrepreneurship.

3. CNN Wire Staff, "Obama Names GE Head to Lead New Economic Council," CNN, January 21, 2011, http://www.cnn.com/2011/POLITICS/01/21/economic .council/index.html.

4. Robert Atkinson, "What's the Right Path for Manufacturing?," *Industry Week,* April 16, 2013, http://www.industryweek.com/innovation/whats-right -path-manufacturing?page=1.

5. Gary Shapiro, "Innovation Not Manufacturing Will Bring Jobs," *Forbes,* March 16, 2011, http://www.forbes.com/sites/garyshapiro/2011/03/16/innovation-not -manufacturing-will-bring-jobs/.

6. Bureau of Labor Statistics, "Employment, Hours, and Earnings from the Current Employment Statistics Survey (National)," http://data.bls.gov/timeseries /CES3000000001?data_tool=XGtable.

7. Mark Boroush, "U.S. R&D Spending Suffered a Rare Decline in 2009 but Outpaced the Overall Economy," National Science Foundation, March 2012, http:// www.nsf.gov/statistics/infbrief/nsf12310/.

8. Hunter Skipworth, "Amazon Set to Sell 8 Million Kindles This Year," *Telegraph,* December 23, 2010, http://www.telegraph.co.uk/technology/news/8219560/A mazon-set-to-sell-8-million-Kindles-this-year.html.

9. "Boiling point? The Skills Gap in U.S. Manufacturing," The Manufacturing Institute and Deloitte, 2011, http://www.nam.org/~/media/A07730B2A798437D 98501E798C2E13AA.ashx.

10. President Barack Obama, 2012 State of the Union Address, January 24, 2012, http://www.whitehouse.gov/the-press-office/2012/01/24/remarks-president -state-union-address.

11. Joe Vardon and Lydia Coutré, "Romney Says He Will Label China a Currency Manipulator," *Columbus Dispatch,* September 26, 2012, http://www.dispatch .com/content/stories/local/2012/09/26/Jack-Nicklaus-endorses-Romney-on -last-day-of-Ohio-bus-tour.html.

12. Mona Mourshed, Diana Farrell, and Dominic Barton, "Education to Employment: Designing a System That Works," McKinsey Center for Government, December 2012, http://mckinseyonsociety.com/education-to-employment/ report/.

13. Richard Vedder, "Why Did 17 Million Students Go to College?" *Chronicle of Higher Education,* October 20, 2010, http://chronicle.com/blogs/innovations /why-did-17-million-students-go-to-college/27634.

14. Kevin Carey, "An Innovative Tech Trio Puts Students in Solid Jobs," *Chronicle of Higher Education,* November 20, 2011, http://chronicle.com/article/An -Innovative-Tech-Trio-Puts/129826/.

15. Bureau of Labor Statistics, "Employment, Hours, and Earnings from the Current Employment Statistics Survey (National)."

16. "2013 Report for America's Infrastructure," American Society of Civil Engineers, March 19, 2013, http://www.infrastructurereportcard.org/a/#p/grade -sheet/americas-infrastructure-investment-needs.

17. Proprietary analysis by Garten Rothkopf.

CHAPTER 7

1. "Monthly Budget Review—Summary for Fiscal Year 2013," Congressional Budget Office, November 7, 2013, https://www.cbo.gov/sites/default/files/447 16-%20MBR_FY2013_0.pdf.

2. "The Debt to the Penny and Who Holds It," TreasuryDirect, U.S. Treasury Department, http://www.treasurydirect.gov/NP/debt/current.

3. "Public Pulse: Does Your Opinion Match the Public's?" Bankrupting America, September 28, 2010, http://www.bankruptingamerica.org/public-pulse-does -your-opinion-match-the-publics/#.VBM6TktFYpE.

4. "The American Recovery and Reinvestment Act," Recovery.gov, http://www .recovery.gov/arra/Pages/default.aspx; "Apollo 11 Moon Landing: Ten Facts about Armstrong, Aldrin and Collins' mission," *Telegraph,* July 18, 2009, http:// www.telegraph.co.uk/science/space/5852237/Apollo-11-Moon-landing-ten -facts-about-Armstrong-Aldrin-and-Collins-mission.html.

5. David Barboza, "Bridge Comes to San Francisco With a Made-in-China Label," *New York Times,* June 25, 2011, http://www.nytimes.com/2011/06/26/business /global/26bridge.html?pagewanted=all.

6. Charles Piller, "Bay Bridge's Troubled China Connection," *Sacramento Bee,* June 8, 2014, http://www.sacbee.com/static/sinclair/sinclair.jquery/baybridge/ #storylink=cpy.

7. Mark Zandi, "Assessing the Macro Economic Impact of Fiscal Stimulus 2008," Moody's Economy.com, January 2008, https://www.economy.com/mark-zandi /documents/Stimulus-Impact-2008.pdf.

8. "Building America's Future: Falling Apart and Falling Behind," Transportation Infrastructure Report 2012, Building America's Future Educational Fund, 2012, http://www.bafuture.org/pdf/Building-Americas-Future-2012-Report-3 2013.pdf.

9. Travis Madsen, Benjamin Davis, and Phineas Baxandall, "Road Work Ahead: Holding Government Accountable for Fixing America's Crumbling Roads and Bridges," U.S. PIRG Education Fund, April 28, 2010, http://www.uspirg.org /reports/usp/road-work-ahead.

10. Charles F. Potts, "Commentary on Infrastructure," *Texas Transportation Researcher* 46, no. 4 (2010): 9, http://d2dtl5nnlpfr0r.cloudfront.net/tti.tamu.edu /documents/researcher/ttr-v46-n4.pdf.

11. "The Fix We're In For: The State of Our Nation's Bridges 2013," Transportation For America, June 19, 2013, http://t4america.org/docs/bridgereport2013/2013 BridgeReport.pdf.

12. Lois Weiss, "Caution: Breath-Holding Zone," *New York Post,* August 8, 2012, http://nypost.com/2012/08/08/caution-breath-holding-zone/.

13. Gerry Smith, "Internet Speed in United States Lags behind Many Countries, Highlighting Global Digital Divide," *Huffington Post,* September 10, 2012,

http://www.huffingtonpost.com/2012/09/05/internet-speed-united-states
-digital-divide_n_1855054.html.

14. "2013 Report Card for America's Infrastructure," American Society of Civil Engineers, March 19, 2013, http://www.infrastructurereportcard.org/.

15. "Failure to Act: The Impact of Current Infrastructure Investment on America's Economic Future," American Society of Civil Engineers, January 15, 2013,
http://www.asce.org/uploadedFiles/Infrastructure/Failure_to_Act/Failure
_to_Act_Report.pdf.

16. "2013 Report Card for America's Infrastructure," American Society of Civil Engineers, March 19, 2013, http://www.infrastructurereportcard.org/.

17. President Barack Obama, "Barack Obama's Acceptance Speech," Democratic
National Convention, Denver, Colorado, August 28, 2008, http://elections.ny
times.com/2008/president/conventions/videos/transcripts/20080828_OB
AMA_SPEECH.html.

18. President Barack Obama, Second Presidential Debate, Nashville, Tennessee,
October 7, 2008, http://www.cnn.com/2008/POLITICS/10/07/presidential.de
bate.transcript/.

19. Office of Inspector General, "Recovery Act: Green Jobs Program Reports
Limited Success in Meeting Employment and Retention Goals as of June 30,
2012," U.S. Department of Labor, October 25, 2012, http://oversight.house
.gov/wp-content/uploads/2012/10/6-30-12-Report-on-Recovery-Act-Green
-Jobs.pdf.

20. "The Green Job Myth," Institute for Energy Research, September 12, 2012,
http://instituteforenergyresearch.org/analysis/the-green-job-myth/.

21. Daniel Steinberg, Gian Porro, and Marshal Goldberg, "Preliminary Analysis of
the Jobs and Economic Impacts of Renewable Energy Projects Supported by the
§1603 Treasury Grant Program," U.S. Department of Energy, April 2012, http://
www.nrel.gov/docs/fy12osti/52739.pdf.

22. Patrice Hill, "'Green Jobs' No Longer Golden in Stimulus," Washington Times,
September 9, 2010, http://www.washingtontimes.com/news/2010/sep/9/green
-jobs-no-longer-golden-in-stimulus/?page=all.

23. Andy Sullivan, "Reuters Analysis: Obama's 'Green Jobs' Have Been Slow to
Sprout," Reuters, April 13, 2012, http://www.reuters.com/article/2012/04/13/us
-usa-campaign-green-idUSBRE83C08D20120413.

24. Hill, "Green Jobs."

25. Sunil Sharan, "The Green Jobs Myth," Washington Post, February 26, 2010,
http://www.washingtonpost.com/wp-dyn/content/article/2010/02/25/AR2
010022503945.html.

26. Barack Obama, "Toward a 21st-Century Regulatory System," Wall Street Journal, January 18, 2011, http://online.wsj.com/articles/SB10001424052748703396
604576088272112103698.

27. "Regulatory Tidal Wave: $515 billion," Small Business for Sensible Regulations,
http://www.sensibleregulations.org/resources/515-billion-dollar-tidal-wave/.

28. Nicole V. Crain and W. Mark Crain, "The Impact of Regulatory Costs on Small Firms," Small Business Association Office of Advocacy, http://www.sba.gov/sites/default/files/advocacy/The%20Impact%20of%20Regulatory%20Costs%20on%20Small%20Firms%20(Full)_0.pdf.
29. Ibid.
30. A job-year is defined as the amount of work equivalent to one year of employment. This could be done by multiple people or one person.
31. "Proposed CATR + MACT," NERA Economic Consulting, prepared for American Coalition for Clean Coal Electricity, May 31, 2011, http://americaspower.org/sites/default/files/NERA_CATR_MACT_29.pdf.
32. "Assessing the Impact of Proposed New Carbon Regulations in the United States," U.S. Chamber of Commerce's Institute for 21st Century Energy, May 2014, http://www.energyxxi.org/epa-regs#.
33. "Steel Industry Reductions in CO_2 Directly Tied to Energy Intensity Reductions," American Iron and Steel Institute, http://www.steel.org/Sustainability/CO2%20Reduction.aspx.
34. "Available and Emerging Technologies for Reducing Greenhouse Gas Emissions from the Iron and Steel Industry," Environmental Protection Agency, September 2012, http://www.epa.gov/nsr/ghgdocs/ironsteel.pdf.
35. "U.S. Trade in Goods and Services-Balance of Payments (BOP) Basis," U.S. Census Bureau, June 4, 2014, http://www.census.gov/foreign-trade/statistics/historical/gands.pdf.
36. "World Energy Outlook 2012," International Energy Agency, November 12, 2012, http://www.worldenergyoutlook.org/publications/weo-2012/#d.en.26099.
37. "Nucor Selects St. James Parish, Louisiana, for Iron-Making Facility," Nucor news release, September 15, 2010, http://www.nucor.com/investor/news/?rid=1471666.

CHAPTER 8

1. "Americans Widely Back Government Job Creation Proposals," Gallup, March 20, 2013, http://www.gallup.com/poll/161438/americans-widely-back-government-job-creation-proposals.aspx.
2. Albert Gallatin, "Report of the Secretary of the Treasury; on the Subject of Public Roads and Canals; made in pursuance of a Resolution of the Senate, of March 2, 1807" (Washington: R.C. Weightman, 1808), http://oll.libertyfund.org/titles/2046; accessed 9/4/2014.
3. F. Delaine Donaldson and Charles Titus, *The Cumberland Road: Individual Rights and Civilization's Advance,* http://www.lib.niu.edu/1995/iht29512.html.
4. Adam Cohen, "Public Works: When 'Big Government' Plays Its Role," Editorial Observer, *New York Times,* November 13, 2007, http://www.nytimes.com/2007/11/13/opinion/13tues4.html?pagewanted=print.

5. "MnDOT celebrated the Interstate High System's 50th Anniversary," Minnesota Department of Transportation, http://www.dot.state.mn.us/interstate50/50facts.html.
6. Wendell Cox and Jean Love, "The Best Investment a Nation Ever Made," Public Purpose, 1996, http://www.publicpurpose.com/freewaypdf.pdf.
7. World Economic Forum, "Global Competitiveness Report 2008–2009," Switzerland, 2008, http://www.weforum.org/pdf/GCR08/GCR08.pdf.
8. World Economic Forum, "Global Competitiveness Report 2012–2013," Switzerland, 2012, http://www3.weforum.org/docs/WEF_GlobalCompetitivenessReport_2012-13.pdf.
9. "Building America's Future: Falling Apart and Falling Behind," Building America's Future Educational Fund, http://www.rockefellerfoundation.org/uploads/files/0d842b6c-aa3a-49d0-b17e-744d3f0d96c7-baf_report.pdf.
10. Ibid.
11. Rep. Peter DeFazio, "Too Little is Spent on Infrastructure," *Politico*, May 13, 2012, http://www.politico.com/news/stories/0512/76245_Page2.html.
12. "Building America's Future," Building America's Future Educational Fund.
13. Tom Evslin, "Everything Is Shovel-Ready in China," *Seeking Alpha*, November 14, 2011, http://seekingalpha.com/article/307638-everything-is-shovel-ready-in-china.
14. Patrick Lyons, "The Bridge to Nowhere Gets Nowhere," *New York Times*, September 21, 2007, http://thelede.blogs.nytimes.com/2007/09/21/the-bridge-to-nowhere-gets-nowhere/.
15. "2012 National Census Population Projections," U.S. Census Bureau, http://www.census.gov/population/projections/data/national/2012.html.
16. Ross DeVol and Perry Wong, "Jobs for America: Investment and Policies for Economic Growth and Competitiveness," Milken Institute, January 2010, http://assets1c.milkeninstitute.org/assets/Publication/ResearchReport/PDF/JFAFullReport.pdf.
17. "2009 Infrastructure Report Card," American Society of Civil Engineers, January 28, 2009, http://www.infrastructurereportcard.org/2009/sites/default/files/RC2009_full_report.pdf.
18. Ibid.; "Failure to Act: The Economic Impact of Current Investment Trends in Water and Waste Treatment Infrastructure," American Society of Civil Engineers, December 15, 2011, http://www.asce.org/Infrastructure/Failure-to-Act/Water-and-Wastewater/.
19. "2009 Infrastructure Report Card," American Society of Civil Engineers; Proprietary Analysis by Garten Rothkopf.
20. FAA NextGen 2012 Implementation Report, http://www.faa.gov/nextgen/media/executive_summary_2012.pdf.
21. "2009 Infrastructure Report Card."
22. "Connecting California 2014 Business Plan," California High Speed Rail Authority, April 30, 2014, http://www.hsr.ca.gov/docs/about/business_plans/BPlan_2014_Business_Plan_Final.pdf.

23. "2011 Statewide Transportation System Needs Assessment," Califronia Transportation Commission, October 2011, http://www.catc.ca.gov/reports/2011 Reports/2011_Needs_Assessment_updated.pdf.
24. David Jackson, "Obama Jokes about 'Shovel-ready Projects,'" *USA Today,* June 13, 2011, http://content.usatoday.com/communities/theoval/post/2011/06/obama-jokes-about-shovel-ready-projects/1#.U_ZCCWSwIzA.
25. Proprietary analysis by Garten Rothkopf.
26. U.S. Department of Transportation Federal Transit Administration Transportation Infrastructure Finance and Innovation Act (TIFIA) program, http://www.fta.dot.gov/grants/12861.html.
27. Proprietary analysis by Garten Rothkopf.
28. "Financial Report 2011," European Investment Bank Group, April 27, 2012, http://www.eib.org/attachments/general/reports/fr2011en.pdf.
29. CalPERS Comprehensive Annual Financial Report: Fiscal Year Ended June 30, 2013, https://www.calpers.ca.gov/eip-docs/about/pubs/cafr-2013.pdf.
30. Randy Diamond, "CalPERS Sets Its Sights on California Infrastructure," Pensions & Investments, October 15, 2012, http://www.pionline.com/article/20121015/ONLINE/121019933/calpers-sets-its-sights-on-california-infrastructure.
31. Ibid.
32. Proprietary analysis by Garten Rothkopf.

CHAPTER 9

1. "World Energy Outlook 2012," International Energy Agency, November 12, 2012, http://www.worldenergyoutlook.org/publications/weo-2012/#d.en.26099.
2. "State of American Energy: America's Energy, America's Choice," American Petroleum Institute, 2014, http://www.api.org/~/media/Files/Policy/SOAE-2014/API-2014-State-of-American-Energy-Report.pdf.
3. "Macroeconomic Impacts of LNG Exports from the United States," NERA Economic Consulting, Prepared for Department of Energy, December 2012, http://energy.gov/sites/prod/files/2013/04/f0/nera_lng_report.pdf.
4. Ken Ditzel, Jeff Plewes, and Bob Broxson, "US Manufacturing and LNG Exports: Economic Contributions to the US Economy and Impacts on US Natural Gas Prices," Charles River Associates, February 25, 2013, http://www.crai.com/uploadedFiles/Publications/CRA_LNG_Study_Feb2013.pdf.
5. James Taranto, "Springtime for Assad," *Wall Street Journal,* December 6, 2012, http://online.wsj.com/news/articles/SB10001424127887324640104578163480051287280.
6. "Second Presidential Debate Full Transcript," *ABC News,* October 16, 2012, http://abcnews.go.com/Politics/OTUS/2012-presidential-debate-full-transcript-oct-16/story?id=17493848&singlePage=true#.UH4eLMXA9gY.

7. Viktoria Steininger, "Groundbreaking Ceremony for New Direct Reduction Plant in Corpus Christi," Voestalpine Corporate Blog, April 24, 2014, http://www.voestalpine.com/blog/en/innovation-en/groundbreaking-ceremony-new-direct-reduction-plant-corpus-christi/.

8. Jack Kaskey, "Shale-Gas Boom Spurs Chilean Methanol Plant's Move to U.S.," Bloomberg, January 18, 2012, http://www.bloomberg.com/news/2012-01-18/shale-gas-boom-spurs-methanex-to-relocate-idled-chilean-plant-to-louisiana.html.

9. "Foreign Direct Investment in Texas 2014: The Countries and Industries Leading Recent Growth," Office of the Governor, 2014, http://governor.state.tx.us/files/ecodev/Foreign_Investment.pdf.

10. "Dow to Build New Ethylene Production Plant at Dow Texas," Dow Chemical Company, press release, April 19, 2012, http://www.dow.com/news/press-releases/article/?id=5646.

11. "Beyond Natural Gas 'Dirty Dangerous and Run Amok,'" Sierra Club, http://content.sierraclub.org/naturalgas/.

12. "Sierra Clubs Natural Gas," Wall Street Journal, May 31, 2012, http://online.wsj.com/news/articles/SB10001424052702304363104577390432521371296.

13. Kevin Begos, "DOE Study: Fracking Chemicals Didn't Taint Water," Associated Press, July 19, 2013, http://bigstory.ap.org/article/ap-study-finds-fracking-chemicals-didnt-spread.

14. Lisa Jackson, "Statement of Lisa Jackson, Committee on Oversight and Government Reform U.S. House of Representatives," May 24, 2011, http://oversight.house.gov/wp-content/uploads/2012/02/5-24-2011_Lisa_Jackson_Full_Committee_Testimony.pdf.

15. "U.S. Energy-related CO2 Emissions in Early 2012 Lowest since 1992," Today in Energy, EIA, August 1, 2012, http://www.eia.gov/todayinenergy/detail.cfm?id=7350.

16. "Greenhouse Gas Inventory Data Explorer," United States Environmental Protection Agency, http://www.epa.gov/climatechange/ghgemissions/inventoryexplorer/#allsectors/allgas/gas/all.

17. "The Economic and Employment Contributions of Shale Gas in the United States," IHS Global Insight, December 6, 2011, http://www.ihs.com/images/Shale_Gas_Economic_Impact_mar2012.pdf.

18. Jerry Burnes, "Hamm: 1 Million Is Just the Beginning," Williston Herald, May 28, 2014, http://www.willistonherald.com/most_recent/hamm-million-is-just-the-beginning/article_9a833b1c-e290-11e3-9358-001a4bcf887a.html.

19. "Eagle Ford Shale: Economic Impact for Counties with Active Drilling," Center for Community and Business Research, The University of Texas at San Antonio, October 2012, http://ccbr.iedtexas.org/.

20. Mark P. Mills, "The International Energy Agency Catches Up with America's Oil Producers," Forbes, November 13, 2012, http://www.forbes.com/sites/markpmills/2012/11/13/530/.

CHAPTER 10

1. U.S. Bureau of Economic Analysis, GDP by Industry Data, http://bea.gov/indus try/gdpbyind_data.htm.
2. Bureau of Economic Analysis, Value Added by Industry as a Percentage of Gross Domestic Product, November 13, 2012, http://www.bea.gov/industry/gdpby ind_data.htm.
3. Bureau of Labor Statistics, "Current Employment Statistics," http://www.bls.gov /ces/.
4. "Facts about Manufacturing," The Manufacturing Institute, November 2012, http://www.themanufacturinginstitute.org/~/media/1242121E7A4F45D68C 2A4586540703A5/2012_Facts_About_Manufacturing___Full_Version___ High_Res.pdf.
5. Proprietary analysis by Garten Rothkopf.
6. Ross DeVol and Perry Wong, "Jobs for America: Investment and Policies for Economic Growth and Competitiveness," Milken Institute, January 2010, http://assets1c.milkeninstitute.org/assets/Publication/ResearchReport/PDF /JFAFullReport.pdf.
7. Sheridan Prasso, "Why We Left Our Factories in China," *Fortune,* June 29, 2011, xhttp://fortune.com/2011/06/29/why-we-left-our-factories-in-china/.
8. Paul Davidson, "Some Manufacturing Heads Back to USA," *USA Today,* August 6, 2010, http://usatoday30.usatoday.com/money/economy/2010-08-06-manu facturing04_CV_N.htm.
9. Ian Fletcher, *Free Trade Doesn't Work: What Should Replace It and Why* (Washington, DC: U.S. Business & Industry Council, 2010).
10. Bureau of Economic Analysis, "Trade in Goods Data Table 2a," http://bea.gov /iTable/iTableHtml.cfm?reqid=6&step=3&isuri=1&600=3.
11. Proprietary analysis by Garten Rothkopf.
12. Bureau of Labor Statistics, "Current Employment Statistics."
13. "Annual Crude Steel Production Archive," World Steel Association, http:// www.worldsteel.org/statistics/statistics-archive/annual-steel-archive.html.
14. Laura Tyson and Greg Linden, "The Corporate R&D Tax Credit and U.S. Innovation and Competitiveness: Gauging the Economic and Fiscal Effectiveness of the Credit," Center for American Progress, January 6, 2012, http:// www.americanprogress.org/issues/tax-reform/report/2012/01/06/10975 /the-corporate-rd-tax-credit-and-u-s-innovation-and-competitiveness/.

INDEX